Jesus Before God

Jesus Before God

THE PRAYER LIFE
OF THE HISTORICAL JESUS

Hal Taussig

POLEBRIDGE PRESS

First Edition

Library of Congress Cataloging-in-Publication Data

Taussig, Hal.
   Jesus before God : the prayer life of the historical Jesus / Hal
Taussig.
      p.   cm.
   Includes bibliographical references and index.
   ISBN 0-944344-75-5
   1. Jesus Christ—Prayers. 2. Jesus Christ—Spiritual life.
3. Jesus Christ—Historicity. 4. Prayer—Christianity. I. Title.
BV229. T38 1999
232.9'5—dc21   99-26930
                                                                            CIP

FOR SUSAN
whose prayer is still growing

CONTENTS

ACKNOWLEDGEMENTS

In the writing of this book I am grateful most of all to my colleagues in the Jesus Seminar. The good-natured rigor of our work together has been the best example I know of scholars working together over a sustained period and has regularly nurtured my own scholarship. How curious our critics sound to us, after our fifteen years of intense study and debate, when they relegate us to the realm of publicity-seeking minor leaguers.

Although it contains a major new scholarly thesis about the historical Jesus' prayer life, this book is intended for the general public. Consequently, I have not included any footnotes. Those interested in the scholarly presentation and supporting footnotes will find them in my recently published profile of the historical Jesus in the scholarly journal *Forum* (1.2, New Series).

I am deeply grateful to Catherine Nerney and Roseann Quinn, my colleagues in the Graduate Program in Holistic Spirituality at Chestnut Hill College, for the dialogue, support, and critique they have provided during this project. Their collegiality and friendship has consistently nurtured me with a nuanced combination of enthusiasm and analysis. Our students and the integrity of their spiritual search and rigorous graduate-level study have provided the context for the final forms of this work.

I am grateful to Char Matejovsky, Bob Funk, Bob Schwartz, and Tom Hall at the Westar Institute for their courage, imagination, and hard work in producing this work.

Finally I am indebted to the congregation of the Chestnut Hill United Methodist Church, whom I serve as pastor, for the wonderful ways they combine intellectual and spiritual search. This combination has helped me remember what is at stake in the broader context of this work.

ABBREVIATIONS

1 Cor	1 Corinthians
Eccl	Ecclesiastes
Ezek	Ezekiel
Gal	Galatians
Isa	Isaiah
Matt	Gospel of Matthew
Ps(s)	Psalm(s)
Q	Sayings Gospel Q
Rom	Romans
Thom	Gospel of Thomas

Introduction

Yes, on second thought it had been a prayer.

It wasn't very much like the prayers any of the others near the meat stall in the village marketplace had heard before. That was obvious from the fact that several were still laughing, a couple others were still scratching their heads, and at least four others were now actively in debate about what had been said.

Actually the incident, which even on third thought still had to be considered some kind of prayer, had all happened so quickly. Hardly anyone had really figured out what was going on until it was over. And even then it was a puzzlement, just because it was still working on those who had been a part of it.

Reconstructing what had happened wasn't all that difficult.

Food had been the main topic of conversation. It was late enough in the day that most of them—the two cloth merchants whose fabrics were spread on the ground, the four farmers and their sons, Jesus and his two traveling companions—were getting hungry. That the meat stall was right across from them reminded them all not only of their momentary hunger, but of the reality that whatever they ate today, it wouldn't include any meat.

Perhaps the vague awareness of yet another meatless day had prompted the sailor to tell a story about a sumptuous meal to which he had been invited three months ago in the banquet hall of the sailor's supper club. There they had not only had fish, but lamb as well. One of Jesus' companions remarked on the sparkle in the sailor's eyes as he spoke of that banquet. But the woman cloth merchant grunted in disgust and resentment, and then brought her complaint to speech: "How come she did not know what she was going to feed her children tomorrow, but the sailors got two different meat dishes!" Others nodded in hungry agreement.

1

One of the farmers then produced a couple of turnips from his bag, and as they talked, he cut them up into small pieces and passed them out to those gathered around. As he passed them out, he said the sailors' banquet didn't bother him as much as just passing by the aristocrats' villas or the Roman soldiers' barracks and smelling the wonderful aromas wafting through the windows. The other merchant and Jesus agreed. The woman traveling with Jesus looked at her piece of turnip and admired the purple pattern on the skin. She held it up beside one of the purple cloths for sale, and smiled. Returning to the farmer's complaint, a son of another farmer grumbled about the way the city folks from Sepphoris to Jerusalem lived off the hard work of the farmers.

A hesitant thought danced at the edge of consciousness among this momentary group in the market square. There was a dim awareness that several of them were not quite sure where the next thing to eat after the piece of turnip would come from. The other companion of Jesus was the first to put it in words. He said to his two traveling partners: "We don't yet have a place to stay tonight." A couple of the farmers knew that they had homes to go to, but weren't quite as sure that everyone there would have enough to eat. The strange mix of the beautiful cloths on the ground, the camaraderie of the conversation, the ache of those not having enough, and the beckoning smells of the marketplace hung tensively in the air.

It was at this moment that it happened—what they would later call "the prayer." Jesus said in a voice that was just audible but with a bit of a rumble, "Give us." He took a deep breath and said, "Give us the bread." He started the sentence again and his two companions said it again with him, "Give us the bread." Jesus' voice was now a little louder as he said, "Give us the bread we need." Now several others of the group said it—not without an edge of anger—with him. Again Jesus spoke, "Give us the bread we need for today." Half out of momentum, his companions and some of the rest of the group said the whole sentence, "Give us the bread we need for today."

By the time that sentence got said a second time, several in the group were laughing at the realization that what they had intended as a demand for bread had turned out to be just as much a challenge to live in the moment. What had started as a plea for justice had also become a call to live fully one day at a time. There was a twinkle in Jesus' eye, another burst of laughter from several people, and a grumpy murmur from a couple of others.

"Just for today? What will we do about tomorrow?" one of the farmer's sons protested.

"Maybe tomorrow will take care of itself," said the sailor.

"You can't ask me to forget about the injustice of our situation," insisted the man selling fabric.

"Look at the birds of the air," said one of Jesus' companions. "God takes care of them just fine."

"Anyway if I can stop worrying for a bit about all of this, it's easier for me to notice the beautiful way the shadows are creeping across the square," said a farmer.

"Well, just how much bread do you think I actually need for today? If I ask just for today, how much is that?" his son retorted.

As the laughter at having been caught saying something one really didn't mean echoed and the discussions proceeded, Jesus and his two companions debated whether to try to find food and lodging for the swiftly approaching night or to take a walk out to the well at the edge of the village. The prayer about the bread kept the debate on the light side. One of the farmers' sons picked up the piece of turnip whose color and patterns complemented the purple cloth, looked at it with a smile, set it back down near the cloth, and murmured to himself "Give us the bread we need for today."

This book is about the prayer life of the historical Jesus. Based within the last twenty years of historical Jesus research, it uncovers an unusual kind of prayer in the life of this Galilean sage. The surprise that awaits the reader may be as unsettling as that experienced by Jesus' audience some two-thousand years ago. How the historical Jesus prayed turns out to be very different from the manner of many of his contemporaries, from the traditional church prayers of today, and from most of the new fashions of contemporary spirituality.

The opening sketch of how and why Jesus may have prayed about "daily bread" is only a hint of a radical shift one needs to make in order to touch the spirit of Jesus' prayer. Discovering the humor and the social character of Jesus' prayer will help greatly in understanding his unusual approach to prayer. But there will be other challenging tasks in making sense of how he prayed and what relevance that has for today's spiritual quests. Several ways of thinking about both prayer and Jesus will have to be challenged in order to find Jesus' own prayer life. Traditional assumptions about what prayer entails, as well as contemporary wish lists of what we need from prayer, will have to be abandoned if a serious search for Jesus at prayer is to be successful.

Opening the Doors

Such a book on Jesus' prayer life would not have been possible a decade ago. In the past ten years two doors have opened, which for most of the twentieth century were bolted shut.

First of all, scholars and the public together have flung open the door to the historical Jesus. For at least the previous two generations, neither biblical scholars nor the public at large have had much interest in the historical person of Jesus, yet now he is a lively subject of much debate and conversation. Many of us in the Jesus Seminar would like to claim credit for this renewed interest in who Jesus was historically. But in a more basic way we must admit that the recent discoveries of new early Christian documents and the emergence of important new methods of reading the evidence have thrust the task of re-thinking the historical Jesus upon us and our entire generation. At any rate, we are now in a time in which weekly news magazines, stodgy professors, national TV, and even the churches all seem engaged by the issue of who Jesus was as an historical person.

Similarly, in stark contrast to much of the modern era, the last decade has blown open the doorway to prayer. As a part of the larger development that is being termed "spirituality," seekers representing a broad spectrum from new age devotees to traditional church-goers are now interested in praying. It is not clear where this renewed passion for prayer has come from. Only a few years ago prayer was considered superstitious by materialists, escapist by social activists, and neurotic by psychologists. But now its effects are being studied by scientists, its power is being sought by burnt-out activists and executives, and its motivation endorsed by therapists.

Given this renewed interest in both the historical Jesus and prayer, several obvious questions move into the foreground. How did Jesus pray? Does the historical human being of first century Galilee named Jesus have something to teach today about prayer? These are the questions at the heart of this book.

A series of second-level questions quickly follow. Was Jesus at heart a wordless mystic? Did he have a special prayer language? Did he pray primarily alone? Did he pray with his followers? Did he use traditional synagogue prayers for his own spiritual expression? How did his teaching relate

Box 1: *What does it mean "to pray?"*

There is a new energy in our time to lend greater meaning both to the words "to pray" and "prayer," and to actions so designated. Everything from the "mindfulness" brought into renewed focus by Buddhist monk Thich Nhat Hanh to the ecstatic speaking in tongues by Christian charismatics seems to apply to the emerging meanings of the concept.

For this book the main definitional terms remain the explicit words for prayer used in Jesus' time and culture. These words and their definitions form the frame of reference for this book's quest for Jesus' own prayer. They also provide a helpful—although not comprehensive—range of meaning for the contemporary search for the significance of praying.

Here are the cluster of Greek words used for praying in Jesus' time:

Proseuchomai (verb) or *Proseuche* (noun)
or *Euchomai* (verb) or *Euche* (noun)

These words are for the overall activity of praying, whether silent or spoken, alone or together. Used very extensively in pagan, Jewish, and Christian literature, they are used both as a "technical term for invoking a deity" (H.Schoenweiss in *Dictionary of New Testament Theology*, ed. Colin Brown) and wordless "nearness of the deity." In non-religious contexts these words mean "to boast, brag, or assert." *Proseuche* can also designate a place for prayer, like a synagogue.

Aiteo (verb) or *Aitema* (noun)

The secular use of this word is much more common than its usage as prayer. The word means to ask or to request. This meaning is occasionally extended to the realm of praying, when it means to request of a deity, that is, to make supplication.

Deomai (verb) or *Deesis* (noun)

This word also generally has a secular meaning of beseeching, which is occasionally extended into the realm of prayer with a similar meaning.

Proskuneo (verb)

The basic meaning of the Greek here is "to kiss." However, this word also became the common term for adoration of the gods. In Jewish, Christian, and pagan literature it is the primary word for worship in a group.

Eucharisteo (verb) or *Eucharistis* (noun)

Used in secular contexts to mean "to give thanks," these words occasionally also take on the meaning of thanking a god. There are several places in the first century of Christian literature—although nowhere in the New Testament—where these words refer to a Christian meal gathering where prayer occurs.

to his own prayer life? Was he interested in everyone using specific formulations like the so-called Lord's Prayer? How did Jesus refer to God in
prayer? The new conversation, both from the perspective of contemporary prayer and historical Jesus research, asks for new categories of inquiry
and new clarity. By the end of the book answers to these questions will
have been presented.

Problems of the Search

For all but the most naïve, making sense of Jesus' prayer life has not
been easy for quite some time now. Understanding how the historical
Jesus prayed has become increasingly difficult on a number of counts. It's
not just that the historical evidence has been practically inscrutable,
although that is true. It is also that in the twentieth century prayer itself
became hard to understand, appearing to be either an obsolete supersti-
tion with no scientific basis or a completely mystified enterprise not subject to common sense or ordinary questions.

In terms of the historical evidence for Jesus' own prayer life, the first
problem has been that the gospels themselves present seemingly contradictory material. Matthew has Jesus instructing people to pray in secret,
while Luke teaches a group of disciples to pray together. In the gospels of
Mark and John Jesus does not teach about prayer at all. In Mark Jesus does
pray, but only in retreat and almost completely without words. In John,
however, Jesus prays an entire chapter worth of prayer with his disciples
and in language completely foreign to the way Jesus talks in Matthew,
Mark, and Luke. In the recently discovered Gospel of Thomas (14:2 and
104:3) Jesus appears to reject outright the proposition that he should pray
at all. In Mark Jesus' only words from the cross are the desperate prayer,
"My God, my God, why did you abandon me?" Yet this picture of Jesus'
prayer on the cross is explicitly contradicted by Luke, who removes the
Markan Jesus' prayer of protest on the cross and replaces it with the confident "Father, into your hands I entrust my spirit."

Other problems of historical evidence make uncovering Jesus' own
prayer life even more complicated. Only two of the gospels contain words
something like "the Lord's Prayer," and these two gospels disagree substantially on the wording. Neither contains all of what what is now
recited as the Lord's Prayer. While there is some superficial agreement
among the canonical gospels about Jesus praying in seclusion, these passages are among the least reliable historically. And, the notion of Jesus

praying in seclusion is at least in tension with the predominance of "we," "us," and "our" in the various versions of the Lord's Prayer.

For those who insist on biblical literalism or on casting a blind eye to all of these evidentiary problems, there is nothing to worry or think about. Those who insist on avoiding any inconsistencies in the Bible either cavalierly pick the passages they like to characterize Jesus' prayer life or naively bunch all of the contradictory behavior into an odd personality for Jesus and call it "divine." But once one asks the question, "What was Jesus' prayer life like?" within a rational perspective, the confusion begins. A coherent portrait of Jesus at prayer does not come easily.

This confusion has been heightened by our own puzzlement about prayer in the twentieth century. Scientific progress in everything from medicine to predicting the weather has made prayer to God for direct control and intervention seem superstitious and unnecessary. Machines and computers now often accomplish tasks and communicate knowledge that people used to think possible only for God. The horrors of the Jewish holocaust, Hiroshima, the Gulag, and the Cambodian holocaust have also raised basic questions for people as to whether God answers prayers anyway. Global awareness of amazing human diversity—both religious and otherwise—has helped bring on a crisis of confidence in what is the right way to pray. All of these factors have undermined previous understandings and practices of prayer, epitomized best perhaps by the prominent theologian Paul Tillich's public withdrawal from prayer in the 1960s, when he said: "I do not pray. I meditate."

To reiterate, both naive acceptance of the gospel accounts of how Jesus prayed and easy assumptions about how to pray have been undercut in our day. Understanding Jesus at prayer has become so problematic that most biblical scholars have abandoned the subject altogether. Because Jesus at prayer confuses theological categories of "divine" and "human" (is there any need for a divine Jesus to pray?), theologians have rarely been interested in Jesus at prayer anyway. Mainstream religious leaders hold desperately to the convention of the Lord's Prayer without addressing the ways it is disappearing from common practice. Meanwhile new spiritualists blithely ignore both Christian tradition and scholarly methodologies comparing Jesus' prayer life to anything from Buddhist meditation to native American vision quests.

Only in the past decade have scholarly breakthroughs in historical Jesus studies and new perspectives on praying itself allowed some of us to begin rethinking what Jesus' prayer life was like.

A New Departure

This book wants to make sense of Jesus at prayer, both in historical terms and for our day. Indeed, it turns out that reconstructing the historical Jesus at prayer and building a contemporary prayer model are one and the same process. A rigorous historical investigation of the early Christian texts—while dismantling a number of traditional images of Jesus' prayer life—produces in these pages a clear picture of the spirituality of the historical person Jesus. While this clear portrait of how Jesus prayed some two-thousand years ago does not answer all the questions and impulses we have today about prayer, it does provide an astonishingly fresh and different model for prayer today.

In chapters ten through fifteen we will examine new ways the historical Jesus can teach us to pray today. The promise of new breakthroughs for prayer today emerges in these final chapters in very surprising forms that burst the molds of most contemporary spirituality. Jesus' prayer life, when applied to western societies in our day, does not fit either traditional church practice or fashionable new spiritual ventures. It turns out to be its own very lively and challenging enterprise, with enormous promise and some of its own limitations. While sketching the promise of contemporary spiritual renewal through Jesus' own prayer, these same chapters also look carefully at the limitations to Jesus' style of prayer for our day.

In other words, the reader must risk thinking new thoughts about both Jesus and prayer. This book's thesis about Jesus' first-century prayer life has been developed during my years as a Fellow of the Jesus Seminar, and was prompted almost entirely by writing assignments I assumed for the Seminar's work and by the rigorous scholarly conversations of the Seminar over the past fifteen years. What follows brings together these various writing assignments and conversations into a portrait of Jesus at prayer.

The Process of Discovery

The search for the historical Jesus at prayer will have its own drama. First attempts at claiming a whole range of gospel pictures of Jesus at prayer will prove disappointing. Eventually some oddly preserved texts will point toward a certain core of historically enticing material. Unfortunately this core will turn out to be fragmented in almost hopeless ways, and in desperate need of re-assembling. In the midst of a painstaking re-assemblage, a surprising shift will occur, uncovering a basic unity to the core material about Jesus at prayer.

Within this drama there is a process for sorting out the material at hand. Discovering the prayer of the historical Jesus involves four stages of investigation.

1. Getting to know the new profile of the historical Jesus. In the last decade a clear profile of the historical Jesus has emerged. In part through the work of the Jesus Seminar and in part as a result of the new documents discovered and the new research methods developed, the historical Jesus' identity seems much clearer than any time in the last century. In the past decade scholars such as John Dominic Crossan, Marcus Borg, Burton Mack, Robert Funk, Kathleen Corley, and Gerald Downing have published major works, which are in basic agreement about who Jesus was. The first stage of discovering Jesus at prayer—detailed in chapter one—entails catching this most recent wave of historical Jesus research.

2. Challenging the assumptions and inherent contradictions in the gospels' portrait of Jesus at prayer. Much of Christian piety has taken all the different references to Jesus at prayer in the four canonical gospels and pasted them together. Unfortunately this has resulted in a very odd picture. For instance, putting the Jesus of John 17's long and ethereal prayer beside Matthew's Jesus, who urges people to pray briefly, plainly, and in secret makes Jesus look either hypocritical or deranged. The second stage of discovering Jesus at prayer—mapped out in an extensive chapter two—examines the texts of Jesus praying and tries to make sense of them. It is in this stage of our investigation that both the Christian patchwork quilt about Jesus at prayer and most of the gospel texts concerning Jesus at prayer will fall apart. For some time during my research of these texts in which I had hoped to find good supportive evidence for Jesus at prayer, it seemed as though nothing clear or positive about Jesus at prayer would emerge. But it was exactly this stage of disintegration that enabled the identification of the new building blocks for an integrated portrait of Jesus at prayer. What at first seemed like fragments of a shattered picture were soon practically begging to show themselves as a part of a new picture. These new prayer fragments emerge in chapters three and four.

3. Hearing the basic prayers of Jesus within the context of his teachings. Once both the pasted together motifs on later Christian piety and the legends of the gospel writers have been removed, there emerges from Jesus a clear and astonishingly fresh voice of prayer. This third stage of the investigation—accomplished in five different chapters (5–9), each devoted to a prayer fragment of the historical Jesus—involves placing these individual prayer fragments of Jesus alongside what else we know about him and his context. The result makes sense of the Jesus who taught and

the Jesus who prayed. By the end of these chapters the prayer life of the historical Jesus will fit more closely with the rest of what we know about him.

4. Assembling a coherent picture of Jesus at prayer. Not only do the prayer fragments match Jesus' teachings, the prayer fragments fit with each other. In this fourth stage the crazy quilt of patchwork piety which has typified most popular images of Jesus will disappear. The strange contradictions produced by trying to take literally the very different descriptions of Jesus at prayer in the gospels are finally replaced. This final stage (chaps. 10–12) will show how the prayer fragments which can be traced to Jesus himself fit together into a much more sensible portrait of a first-century teacher at prayer. Although this new picture will eliminate most of the problems encountered when one tries to take the various gospels literally and pasted together, it will be a surprising picture. How Jesus prayed will turn out to be quite different from what we expected.

Implications for Today

By way of conclusion, chapters 13–15 will lay the contemporary quest for enlivened prayer at the feet of the historical Jesus. What we have learned about Jesus' prayer we will bring to bear on today's longings for re-connection to the divine, on the various new impulses toward spirituality, and on the twentieth-century's quandaries about prayer.

This will be a relatively unsentimental application of Jesus' prayer to our day. While taking seriously the fresh approach to spirituality evident in the historical Jesus, these chapters will honor both the possibilities and the limitations inherent in Jesus' prayer. The final movement of this book means to find real help from the historical Jesus for today's praying without pretending that the spirituality of a first century Galilean peasant is all that is needed for people at the turn of the second millennium. A basic honesty about both the historical Jesus and the complexities of spiritual consciousness today will guide us. Such honesty will point us toward new insights from Jesus about how to pray as well as suggest where we need to look to non-Jesus-related resources for contemporary spiritual development.

It is my hope that by the end of this book the reader will have discovered a much clearer picture of the historical Jesus at prayer, some fresh impulses from Jesus for prayer today, and courage to unfold their own powerful spiritual practice.

1
A New Portrait
of Jesus

The twentieth century—especially in its final decades—has brought the historical person, Jesus of Nazareth, into much clearer focus. The scholarly effort which began in the eighteenth century to sort out historically reliable information about Jesus from legend now makes the cover of weekly secular news magazines. Although some parts of the public are actively resisting this new information, much of the public no longer takes the gospels naively as direct reports of what happened in the life of Jesus. In the past two decades both new scholarly breakthroughs and increased public discussion have accelerated the pace of learning about the historical Jesus.

This chapter is a summary of what the twentieth century has learned about the historical Jesus. The summary is presented with two special concerns. First of all, it is important that the reader understand both what the new picture of Jesus is and how the new picture has come about. This chapter wants to trace the basic evidence and logic of the current understanding of the Jesus of history. Secondly, the summary will concentrate on the parts of the current portrait which elucidate our primary quest for information about the prayer life of Jesus.

A STORY

The food had been cleared away, and the dogs had been let into the room to eat up the scraps on the floor. Wine, although not the best, was now being passed out to those on the straw-covered, wooden couches around the room. And, as the conversation began in earnest, the first topics were the usual review of what had gone on in the village in the past several weeks. Several of the farmers were wondering why the corner of the new addition to the bakery had collapsed.

"Didn't they use the right materials?" one of them wondered.

11

"Well, in any case somebody wasn't paying attention," said another. And several others chimed in about the importance of doing one's work well.

"I just think good work is a sign of God working with us. You can probably tell how close persons are to God by how well they do their work," the tailor's eldest son said.

It was at that point that one of the wandering sages on a couch in the corner spoke: "There was this sower from a village down the way, who went out to do his job one day. He just started throwing the seed around. Some of the seed landed along the path, and before he was finished the birds were already eating it all up. Other seed fell on rocky ground, where there wasn't much soil. So, as you can imagine, that seed sprouted very quickly in the thin layer of soil. But when the sun came out, within a day, the little plants had withered, since they really had no roots. And some of the rest of the seed fell among the thorns, which choked the plants so that they could not really produce."

At this point a couple of the farmers had started laughing at what a bad job this sower was doing. One of them yelled out, interrupting the story: "Where did this guy learn to plant seed?"

The sage in the corner—someone said his name was Jesus, and that he was from Nazareth, the village across the valley—shook his head in agreement, laughed with them, and continued his story: "Well, actually some of the seed did land on some good soil. That seed produced. In fact, one section produced thirty times the amount of seed, a second section produced sixty times the amount, and a third section produced one-hundred times the amount."

"You mean, after all that screw-up in planting, there was a great crop?" one of the younger farmers asked.

"I don't know," said Jesus, smiling, "it's just a story."

"But it's surprising," said one of the baker's friends, "I would have never thought that it would turn out that way. It sounds as if doing a good job isn't the only way to happy endings."

Three people responded to that thought at once, and soon there were several conversations going on among the twenty three men in the room. One group continued the debate about whether it was important always to do your best work. Another group kept up the focus on what the baker was going to do now that his new room had collapsed. A smaller group, consisting of two other wandering sages and a cloth merchant, mused about whether God cared about the results of work. They were in the opposite corner from the Nazarene, and at one point yelled across the dining room to him, "So, guy from Nazareth, what do you think about God? Is God in our work?"

The Nazarene, looking a bit unkempt, took a sip of wine and spoke up, so that the group across the room could hear: "God rules this way. A woman took yeast, and mixed it with a whole bunch of flour until it was all leavened."

More laughter. More scratched heads. A good deal of delight.

"How can you compare God to what a woman does? And yeast, that's impure too. What a crazy comparison! The next thing you'll be comparing God to children."

Again the gathering, momentarily convened by Jesus' loud voice shouting from one corner of the room to the other, broke up into different groups of couches discussing different topics.

A Sage

All the major scholars of our day agree that Jesus was a sage. This scene is based upon the emerging consensus that Jesus' primary historical identity was that of a sage. In the first-century Mediterranean cultures a sage was someone devoted to wisdom. That is, a sage was interested both in understanding life and in communicating that understanding. These near eastern devotees of wisdom were eager to learn life's secrets and to help others do the same.

In the past fifteen years of scholarship Jesus as sage has become the key to understanding who he was. Everyone from the evangelical Ben Witherington (whose recent book is called *Jesus the Sage*) to the relentlessly critical Burton Mack make Jesus as sage the central concept. Perhaps the best cases for this way of looking at Jesus have been made by John Dominic Crossan (in his popular *Jesus: A Revolutionary Biography*, and in his voluminous *The Historical Jesus*) and Marcus Borg (in the well-written book for lay people, *Meeting Jesus Again for the First Time*, and in his more scholarly *Jesus: A New Vision*).

The Jesus Seminar, the much-publicized group of some one hundred New Testament scholars, emphasized Jesus as sage in *The Five Gospels*, its first major report on its findings about the historical Jesus: "The sage of the ancient Near East was laconic, slow to speech, a person of few words. The sage does not provoke encounters … As a rule, the sage is self-effacing, modest, and unostentatious" (32).

Newly available material (see Boxes 2 and 3, pp. 15–16) about Jesus as sage has made it clear that Jesus belonged to this large near eastern search for wisdom during the Greco-Roman period. These earliest layers of texts about Jesus contained little except teachings of Jesus. These layers— newly in focus thanks to both new documentary discoveries and break-throughs in understanding how the gospels were written—contained lit-tle about what Jesus did. The Gospel of Thomas, the Gospel of Q, and the pre-gospel collections of parables were collections of sayings by Jesus with the barest of context. There was no story of Jesus' life in these collections. In fact there were not even stories about Jesus doing anything in these earliest sources. These earliest layers contained only various forms of wis-dom sayings. They were basically collections of the sayings of the sage Jesus.

Since they were, as noted earlier, devoted to communicating their understanding of life, we can clearly consider these Mediterranean sages to have been teachers. That is why it is quite conceivable that Jesus was called "Rabbi" in the villages of Galilee, where he lived. During the early part of the first century when Jesus lived, "Rabbi" was not a technical term for a synagogue official. It simply meant "teacher."

But as a sage, Jesus was not simply a teacher. He spent at least as much time in figuring things out himself as in communicating the understand-ing he came to. Jesus as teacher devoted himself to the more basic task of seeking wisdom, a task in which he fervently believed. "There is nothing veiled that won't be unveiled or hidden that won't be made known," a saying attributed to Jesus in six different early Christian texts, shows this confidence Jesus had in the possibility of figuring things out and then say-ing what he understood.

The best place to gain wisdom, according to Jesus the sage, was right in the midst of ordinary life. In interacting with the Roman soldier who forced you to carry his pack for a mile, in the way field workers got hired and paid, in the way lilies grew in the field, and in the way a woman made bread, one could discover wisdom. Jesus' sayings from the earliest layers of the gospels and in the newly discovered documents have a clear focus on everyday life as the place to be, if one really wants to be both wise and holy.

This concentration on everyday life meant that Jesus as a sage did not emphasize either holy scriptures or established religious systems as privi-leged sources of wisdom. The sayings of Jesus in the earliest layers of evi-dence do not show Jesus quoting the Hebrew Bible with any regularity. Instead he taught about the blessedness of the poor or the way the domain of God was perceivable in a mustard seed growing. Rather than pointing to traditional texts Jesus pointed to the birds of the air, the employment practices of farmers, the goings on in the marketplace, the

**Box 2: Recently Discovered Documents
about Jesus Outside the Bible**

The Didache
    Also known as The Teaching of the Twelve Apostles, this is a complete
document, which instructs early Christian communities on how to behave
and how to do certain early Christian rituals, such as baptism and
eucharist. Discovered in 1875 and the topic of a number of recent studies,
it was probably written first near the end of the first century C.E. and then
revised in the early second century.

The Gospel of Mary
    An extensive fragment discovered in Egypt at the end of the nineteenth
century, but only properly translated and published in the latter half of the
twentieth century. It features teachings of Jesus and of his close disciple
Mary Magdalene. Probably written around 125 C.E.

The Gospel of Peter
    An extensive fragment found in Egypt in the 1860s, telling a story of
Jesus' arrest, crucifixion, and resurrection. Probably written in the latter
half of the first century.

The Gospel of Thomas
    A complete gospel of 114 sayings of Jesus, discovered in Egypt in 1945.
It contains many sayings found in the biblical gospels and many not found
in any other documents. Its discovery confirmed the existence of so-called
"sayings gospels," which contain only Jesus' teachings and not any deeds.
Probably written somewhere between 50 and 125 C.E.

Oxyrhynchus Papyrus 1
    A fragment from an ancient Egyptian trash heap, containing five com-
plete sayings of Jesus from the Gospel of Thomas and portions of four
other Jesus teachings from the Gospel of Thomas.

Oxyrhynchus Papyrus 654

    A fragment of forty-two lines discovered around the beginning of the
twentieth century in Egypt, containing the introduction and first five sayings of the Gospel of Thomas. Clearly from a different source than
Oxyrhynchus Papyrus 1.

Oxyrhynchus Papyrus 655
    Eight small scraps of a scroll containing five sayings of Jesus, discovered
around the turn of the twentieth century. The five sayings are very similar to Gospel of Thomas 36–40, but the script is different from both 654
and 1.

Box 3: Pre-gospel Documents about Jesus
Identified by Twentieth-Century Literary Investigations

The Q Gospel
   A collection of some 240 versus of sayings of Jesus which eventually
found their way into the Gospels of Matthew and Luke. See a longer
explanation of this crucial document in the search for the prayer of the
historical Jesus in chapter three.

A Pre-Gospel Collection of Parables
   A series of parables and interpretations of parables linked together in
writing, which the Gospel of Mark eventually placed in its fourth chapter
and then added its own interpretations.

A Chain of Miracle Stories
   A set of six or seven stories about Jesus' healing, feeding throngs of people, and walking on water, modeled after both the miracle stories of Elijah
and Elisha and the story of the Exodus. This "chain" eventually found its
way into the Gospels of Mark, Matthew, and Luke.

The Signs Gospel
   Another collection of miracle stories about Jesus, bound fairly tightly
together by the interpretation that Jesus performed miracles as signs that
he was the Messiah. This small gospel was taken over by and integrated
into the Gospel of John.

---

work of women in the household, and the social life of the peasant as the
real sources of wisdom and authority.

   Nor do the earliest documents of Jesus' teachings portray him as having much cared about religious institutions, religious systems of thought
or belief, or religious codes of behavior. There are no sayings from Jesus in
these early layers about the Temple in Jerusalem, either for or against it.
Most scholars think that when Jesus finally went to Jerusalem, he did per-
form some action meant to criticize the Temple; but scholars do not agree
at all on what that action was. The saying imbedded in the texts about
Jesus in the Temple looks too much like part of an ancient story-telling
device to be a reliable record of what Jesus said.

   Nor did Jesus' teachings go out of their way to promote basic aspects of
Jewish faith. It is easy to see in these early teachings that Jesus assumed
the main tenets of Jewish faith. The oneness of God, the high ethical
standards associated with Judaism, the Jewish concern for fairness and justice, and God's active role in the governance of the world are all affirmed
in Jesus' teachings. He seems to have assumed that Judaism as a faith was

God's way, and then concentrated on expanding ways of understanding one's self and God within that frame. The real energy of his teachings is found in their expansiveness of vision and in their critique, not in their defense, of religion. Typical of Jesus' stance toward the religious systems in place is the parable that saw God's domain in the actions of a social outsider like a Samaritan rather than in those of a priest.

Nor did Jesus' teachings encourage people to follow religious codes of behavior. It is important to acknowledge that in all the gospels—both in the passages where we find Jesus' original teachings and in the texts where the gospel writers have gone beyond his original actions and teachings—there is never a place where Jesus placed himself outside of Judaism. Also since Jesus clearly affirmed himself as belonging to Judaism, it is inaccurate to see Jesus as having campaigned systematically against religious or specifically Jewish religious behavior. But the cutting edge of his teachings often calls some of these religious behaviors into question. Perhaps the best example of the way this Jewish sage pushed people to seek a deeper understanding rather than blindly following religious rules is his teaching about the sabbath: "The sabbath day was created for Adam and Eve, not Adam and Eve for the sabbath day." Here Jesus did not denigrate the sabbath, he just tried to put it in the larger context of his search for wisdom, the context of the created world and of ordinary experience.

In both the Jewish and Greco-Roman settings of Jesus' time, there were plenty of examples of this kind of sage. The biblical books of Proverbs and Ben Sirach are collections of the sayings of various sages about everything from raising children to protocol in the king's court. For instance, the sage wrote in Ben Sirach 6:15, "A loyal friend is something beyond price, there is no measuring the price of such friendship." Some of these teachings, however, with their emphasis on lessons to be learned from life apparently began to wear thin. "Koheleth" produced a collection of sayings in the book of Ecclesiastes which questioned how much wisdom can really be found. So, for instance, in 9:18 and 10:1, this sage observed, "Wisdom is worth more than weapons of war, but a single sin undoes a good deal of good. One dead fly can spoil the scent-maker's oil; a grain of stupidity outweighs wisdom and glory." But even in his skepticism, Koheleth kept the sage's focus on everyday life and on the possibility of life revealing at least some wisdom ("Better to be a live dog than a dead lion," Eccl 9:4). Whether skeptical, conventional, or innovative, the sage looked for wisdom in life itself. It was not in sacred texts or institutions that wisdom was revealed. It was in the discipline of being present to what one lived.

Similarly, the sages of the Stoic and Cynic movements, popular at the time of Jesus, concentrated on life experiences as the place where real wisdom was discernible. Mack, Crossan, and Gerald Downing have all produced major works which make extensive and successful comparisons between Jesus and especially the popular Cynic sages of that day. The Roman writer Lucian, cited by Crossan, described the way the second-century C.E. sage Demonax "led the same life and ate the same food as everyone else, was not in the least subject of pride, and played his part in society and politics." The Cynic philosophers, who intentionally dressed in demonstratively simple ways, were especially well-known for hanging around the market places and any banquet they could find their way into in order both to gain and disperse wisdom.

Jesus taught in these same places. His favorite place to teach was probably at dinner. Jesus seems to have been so closely associated with dinners that an early criticism of him was that he was "a glutton and a drunkard, a friend of tax collectors and sinners" (Matt 11:19). As Kathleen Corley has shown in her book *Private Women, Public Meals*, these dinners were usually semi-private. Perhaps the word "banquet" better suggests who attended these meals. They were hosted by an individual, family, club, or organization and held either in a rented room or the home of an aristocrat. These meals were quite common, and provided important occasions for socializing in the Mediterranean world.

There is very little evidence of Jesus himself hosting a meal. The gospels consistently portray him as a guest. When the gospels have him speak at a meal, he almost always does so as a guest among other guests. Such was the normal order of affairs at meals in the Mediterranean culture of that day, with various sages, entertainers, and musicians contributing. Jesus as guest sage also fits well with the relative shortness of all of Jesus' sayings found in the earliest layers of evidence. As a guest, Jesus was probably not sufficiently in control of the situation to have spoken at length. In passages like the "sermon on the mount" the gospel story line calls for Jesus to present a longer set of teachings, but the clumsy way the sayings in these longer "sermons" bump up against one another is evidence that it was the gospel writers who patched together a series of sayings, rather than Jesus who repeated them one after another. As we will see when we examine the specific kinds of punch-line related teachings of Jesus, his wisdom was particularly suited to short presentations.

Sages in this part of the Near East wandered from village to village, carrying practically nothing with them as a visible sign that all they needed in life was the wisdom they offered and sought. Such a strategy is found in the Gospel of Thomas' rendering of an early saying of Jesus: "When you go into any region and walk about in the countryside, when people take you in, eat what they serve you" (14:4). That this was a rather general behavior of all kinds of sages is shown in this quotation from Epictetus:

> I wear a rough cloak even as it is, and I shall have one then; I have a hard bed even now, and so I shall then; I shall take to myself a wallet and a staff, and I shall begin to walk around and beg from those I meet.
> —*Discourses* 3.22:9, 10

Not Just Any Sage

As scholars of the last twenty years have zeroed in on the problem of which sayings attributed to Jesus in the ancient literature may have actually been said by him and which were added by his followers for various purposes, Jesus has emerged as a rather astonishing sage. Scholars have noticed, for instance, a number of sayings which occur in a variety of independent pieces of literature, and therefore may be quite close to what Jesus himself said. On the other hand, it has become relatively clear that some other sayings reveal views of the later gospel writers, and as such are probably not from Jesus. In these and other ways the research of this century has been able to identify a core group of teachings by the historical Jesus which are consistently fresh, funny, and insightful.

These sayings closest to Jesus of Galilee bubbled over with surprise. They stood conventional wisdom on its head. For instance, the standard wisdom that wealth is a sign of God's blessing became in the mouth of Jesus the ironic and liberating, "Blessed are the poor." Or, the way God acts got compared in a single pithy sentence to both a woman at work in her household and the yeast which most of the culture considered impure.

Jesus' teachings astonished his hearers. When he spoke, people were likely to be either inspired or outraged at the way he broke through conventional thinking and behavior. The pithy and provocative sayings found in the earliest collections of his teachings targeted accepted ways of doing things in a style that surely disturbed some and encouraged others. One of the primary methods in Jesus' search for wisdom was to learn by challenging and debunking convention. He seemed to assume that if one called into question old habits and norms, something far more fresh and powerful could be unveiled.

Three conventional institutions came in for the most critique by Jesus: family, wealth, and religion. Against none of these did he mount a thorough-going attack. Rather he targeted the pretensions of these institutions without directly calling for any systematic reform. His strategy, it seems, was to help people see how funny some of these assumptions made them and everyone else look. He called the privileges of blood ties and ability to produce children into question. In a context where family loyalty was the equivalent of social security, he said:

> "My mother and my brothers—who ever are they? Here are my mother and brothers. For whoever does the will of my Father in heaven, that's my brother and sister and mother."　　　　　　　　　　—Matt 12:48–50

In a social situation where having children was perhaps a man's greatest source of status, Jesus said:

> "There are castrated men who castrated themselves because of Heaven's imperial rule."　　　　　　　　　　　　　　　　—Matt 19: 12

He mocked the ways the affluent received and bankrolled prestige:

> "Congratulations, you poor! God's domain belongs to you."　—Luke 6:20

In the face of the status value of accumulated wealth, surely with a smile he tweaked people's ambitions with:

> "If you have money, don't lend it at interest. Rather, give it to someone from whom you won't get it back."　　　　　　　　　—Thom 95:1, 2

And he challenged those who were "holier than thou":

> "Be on guard against the scholars who like to parade around in long robes, and who love to be addressed properly in the marketplaces, and who prefer important seats in the synagogues and the best couches at the banquets."
> 　　　　　　　　　　　　　　　　　　　　　　　—Luke 20:46

With reference to religious prescriptions about what to eat and what not to eat (and most likely with reference to people defecating), he said:

> "It's not what goes into a person from the outside that can defile; rather it's what comes out of a person that defiles."　　　　　　—Mark 7: 15

One of the main ways Jesus identified what emerged when the pretenses of conventional family, wealth, and religion were dropped was what he called the "domain of God." Interestingly enough, the "domain of God"—like real wisdom—was present for Jesus in the daily pursuits of life like the household, the marketplace, and the countryside. In the very same places where family, wealth, and religion claimed privilege, underneath the pretense one could find "God's domain."

Between 20 and 25 percent of the sayings attributed to the historical

Jesus by the Jesus Seminar make reference to this "domain of God." The way Jesus' core teachings presented this notion was fresh and evocative. God's domain became something that the poor inherited. It was like the way seeds grew into plants which then produced a harvest. God's way of acting ended up—through the lens of Jesus' teachings—looking like that of children (Matt 18:3 and parallels in Mark and Luke).

Jesus seemed to be suggesting that God's domain was present in unexpected ways. The Gospel of Thomas shows Jesus describing God's domain as "spread out upon the earth, and people don't see it" (113:4). Nor was God's domain just in heaven or in the future. It was—for those "with ears to hear"—like an open dinner invitation, and as visible as a city set on a mountain or a light uncovered.

Since wisdom from everyday life was easily uncovered and God's domain was available at every turn for the discerning ear or eye, Jesus taught that one need not worry about the basics of life. "God causes the sun to rise on both the bad and the good, and sends rain on both the just and the unjust" (Matt 5:45). That one could trust God's care was obvious in the birds of the air or the lilies of the field. And, one could therefore risk much more and be free of dependency on riches, family, and status. One could also put in perspective the claims of the Roman empire, which ruled all of the Mediterranean world and completely dominated what used to be the nation of Israel.

On this subject consider for a moment the phrase so frequently occurring in Jesus' teachings, "basileia tou theou," (which we have been translating, "God's domain," following the translation in the recent *The Complete Gospels: Annotated Scholars Version*, ed. Robert Miller, and which has traditionally been translated "kingdom of God." Other recent helpful translations are "reign of God" and "God's imperial rule.") This phrase is really yet another clever taunt by Jesus. Whenever anyone in Jesus' time used the term "basileia" (or "kingdom"), the first thing people thought of was the Roman "kingdom" or "empire." That is, "basileia" really meant "Roman empire" to most people who heard it. So, when Jesus taught about the "basileia" of God, he was mocking the pretense of the Roman empire in a subtle, but unmistakable, way. He was calling into question the presumption of his hearers that Rome was in charge, and calling for them to entertain the idea of how life could be lived through the vision of God's domain, "spread out upon the earth" that people generally didn't see.

This is why the other translation of "basileia tou theou" in the *Scholars Version* "God's imperial rule" captures the flavor of Jesus' clever taunt. A rendering which might pick up the taunt even more explicitly would be to talk about "God's empire." The satire implicit in Jesus' first-century teachings about this "basileia/imperial rule" might be similar to someone in the late twentieth century talking about "God's multi-national corporation" as a way of tweaking the pretentiousness and domination of today's multi-national corporations.

Although "God's imperial rule" or "God's empire" do illustrate nicely the taunt against Rome in all Jesus' "kingdom" sayings, these two new translations are ultimately more confusing than helpful. In today's America they unintentionally evoke the notion of a Christian empire ruling the world. When the general populace today read of Jesus talking about an empire, a natural (but disastrously mistaken) interpretation is that Jesus predicted and endorsed the western Christian empire-like domination of the world today. The historical Jesus clearly was not interested in endorsing a class of pious wealthy westerners of our day in their quest for world domination. If anything, he would have been skewering the pretense of western Christian domination over everyone else as thoroughly as he debunked the pretensions of Rome and Jerusalem in his day.

Jesus' teachings about God's reign were fresh and surprising. But the idea of a sage talking about a new kind of "kingdom" resulting from the search for wisdom was not new. As both John Dominic Crossan and Burton Mack have shown, many sages couched their search for wisdom in terms suggesting that wise people are the true kings. Among many quotes cited by Crossan from other sages of Jesus' time, consider the following:

> Look at me, who am without a city, without a house, without possessions, without a slave; I sleep on the ground; I have no wife, no children, no praetorium, but only the earth and heavens, and one poor cloak... Am I not free? When did any of you see me failing in the object of my desire? Or ever falling into that which I would avoid?... any of you ever see me with sorrowful countenance? And how do I meet with those whom you are afraid of and admire? Do not I treat them like slaves? Who, when he sees me, does not think that he sees his king and master?
> —Epictetus, *Discourses* 3.22:45–49, *Oldfather* 2.146–147

So the use of kingdom/domain language by Jesus to describe what happens in search for wisdom was something he shared with many other sages.

In this regard Jesus' teachings maintained a creative tension between the socio-political and economic concerns of his day and the search for wisdom. Since Jesus used terms that evoked thoughts about Rome, the distribution of wealth, and the bias in family systems, it is impossible to say that he disregarded politics and economics in his search for wisdom. But neither did he become a social or economic reformer. He seemed to encourage people to think actively about socio-political and economic matters, and then to concentrate on integrating those insights into a fresh and wisdom-filled way of living.

This wisdom-oriented approach to politics and economics by no means points to an other-worldly emphasis. Just because Jesus' teachings don't reflect an explicit effort to reform or revolutionize the political and economic systems doesn't indicate that he sought a wisdom removed from the world in which he lived. As we have seen, almost all of the early sayings of Jesus concentrate on this-worldly topics. Nor was his wisdom-oriented political stance similar to current American individualism, which makes light of social concerns. Many of Jesus' teachings—in their own humorous and fresh way—focus on social interactions. Because the teachings of Jesus critiqued a great deal of social convention and asked his hearers to develop a less superficial relationship with life itself, it is fair to characterize this wisdom-based approach as a spiritual one. But Jesus' wisdom spirituality had a clear social and this-worldly orientation.

So Jesus was no ordinary sage. His teachings were so striking that usually his hearers were inspired, shocked, or actively puzzled. When he spoke, the clever social involvement of his teachings called people to self-examination and new relationships. This kind of wisdom teaching, which draws the hearers into new ways of understanding beyond that of either common proverbs or conventional expectations, has been named "aphoristic." Robert Funk summarizes a decade of scholarship on aphoristic teaching by contrasting it to proverbial wisdom: "An aphorism, on the other hand, is a subversive adage or epigram: it contradicts or undermines folk wisdom….Folklore, or proverbial wisdom, reflects the regnant sensibilities of a people. Aphorisms contravene that sensibility and endeavor to replace the old perception with new" (Honest to Jesus, 136).

The teachings of Jesus were then for the most part ground-breaking. But what can we say of his audience? It is important first to remember that all the early sayings we have from Jesus were short. For the great majority of scholars, the long speeches Jesus gives in the Gospel of John are not historical. The gospels of Matthew, Mark, Luke, and Thomas contain no such long speeches, and the content of Jesus' teachings in John is so different from that in the other gospels. We have noted earlier how this evidence that Jesus taught in brief sayings fits with the common practice of sages as guest teachers at banquets. We also know from ancient Mediterranean literature that small schools often met in marketplaces.

This raises questions about the historical accuracy of the occasional pictures of Jesus teaching large crowds. Since the settings that make most sense for Jesus' teaching are the smaller venues, those stories about Jesus addressing large crowds are probably later legend. It is also probably not accidental that most of the stories about Jesus teaching large crowds have other symbolic and legendary characteristics (like feeding five thousand people or walking on water).

Just because Jesus probably taught more in settings of ten to fifty supper guests or in marketplaces does not mean that he was little known in his day. It simply means he became known in the same way other sages of his day did. It seems clear that his fresh teachings made him a premiere teacher of Galilee in his day.

Not the Messiah

As we have noticed, the earliest documents about Jesus' life give evidence that his teaching made a strong impression on the Galileans to whom he spoke. The impressive response Jesus received is attested by an interesting succession of written evidence. The first documents we have from the Galilean milieu—the sayings gospels of Thomas and Q and the pre-gospel collections of parables found, for example, in Mark 4—are typically composed of short wisdom sayings. These are clearly efforts to record, imitate, and expand on the wisdom his followers heard in his pithy teachings. His teachings clearly sparked others in a search for wisdom and an attention to the domain of God.

The next stages of written evidence reveal a layer of lore and legend developing around him. By lore and legend, I mean the material in the early Christian literature which pro-actively went beyond what might have happened to create enhanced pictures of Jesus. These enhanced pictures of Jesus generally made him more powerful and more relevant to the particular setting of the later gospel writers. Even Q and Thomas in their later stages of composition have started making Jesus into something more than a sage. The Gospel of Thomas took one of the most obvious steps by portraying him as the mythical figure of Wisdom herself. In Thomas, for instance, Jesus not only spoke of the subtle presence of God's domain, Jesus became that presence. Similarly the latter stages of Q wrote Jesus into a dialogue with Satan, where Jesus is pitted in legendary fashion against the chief of evil. Then the crucial stage of creating the legends of Jesus occurred when Mark wrote the first gospel that was an extended story of Jesus from the beginning of his ministry to his resurrection. Matthew, Luke, and John followed suit.

A crucial means by which the Christian gospels expressed the unique character of Jesus was to call him the "Messiah." The Greek word for Messiah, "Christ," was used as early as the letters of Paul in the 50s. So at least by the second generation of Jesus' followers, "Messiah" or "Christ" became a way of people claiming him as their special symbol and/or leader. Because these relatively early documents called Jesus Messiah and because all four of the biblical gospels emphasized that Jesus was the Messiah one might expect that either Jesus himself or at least those around him proclaimed him as the Messiah.

That would, however, be a mistake. There are three very striking evidentiary reasons to question the historical accuracy of the followers of Jesus calling him the Messiah during his lifetime:

1. The earliest documents about Jesus' life, namely the gospels of Q and Thomas, have no teachings by Jesus about his being the Messiah. In fact, in neither of these early gospels is there even a mention of the Messiah. The fact that they do not even allude to Jesus as Messiah is a strong indication that seeing Jesus as Messiah was a later idea.

2. What we know about Jesus' life does not correspond to the definition of Messiah. "Messiah" is the title given to the king expected by many Jews to come at the end of the age. The Messiah/king was to restore Israel to its nationhood and make Israel a righteous and powerful expression of God's will. The problem in matching up Jesus with the Messiah title is obvious. All the early portraits of Jesus—even the most legendary—did not describe Jesus as a king. In the gospels, both early and late, Jesus was a teacher, prophet, and/or miracle worker. He was never portrayed as a king. Even if we give credence to some obviously legendary material about who Jesus was, there are no pieces of literature at all from the first century which show him as a political leader, much less someone who is the last king of Israel, who establishes Israel as powerful nation once again. Everyone knew that Jesus neither restored Israel nor became its last king.

The idea of Jesus being Messiah could be proposed only in the generations after he lived as legends about him grew. Even then, the idea was a stretch or at least an odd metaphor, since it was clear to all that he had been executed by the Romans. That would not have happened to the true Messiah.

In an odd way the biblical gospels actually reflect the lack of early evidence for Jesus as Messiah. Although in Matthew, Mark, and Luke Jesus was clearly proclaimed as the Messiah, none of these gospels dared record Jesus actually proclaiming himself as the Messiah. Peter so acclaims him and in some places evil spirits call him "Son of God," which may have been a messianic title. In the stories of the trial of Jesus before the Sanhedrin the question comes up as to whether Jesus is the Messiah. Only in Mark—and there only once—does Jesus answer, "I am" to the question about his identity as the Messiah. In Matthew and Luke, Jesus seems to avoid or deflect the question. Even in the gospels of Matthew and Luke, who openly promoted Jesus as Messiah, Jesus never so identifies himself. That others in all three of these gospels acclaim Jesus as the Messiah (Peter, evil spirits, the crowd)—while Jesus does not—is most probably an indication that the gospel writers knew that naming Jesus "the Messiah" did not fit with either what the historical Jesus taught or with the normal definition of Messiah.

Since the historical Jesus' life fit so poorly with the title of Messiah, scholars have wondered for the past two centuries how the idea of Jesus as Messiah got started. It could be that early Christians after Jesus' death fit him into apocalyptic scenarios about the end of the world. There are hints of this in the way that Paul—who never met the historical Jesus— wrote about him. On the other hand, there is some indication that Peter, James and a group of Jesus' followers moved from Galilee to Jerusalem sometime after Jesus' death. Such a move to Jerusalem to continue Jesus' legacy would almost certainly have been intended to give the movement socio-political importance by moving it to the capital city of ancient Israel. Such a move to Jerusalem to highlight the religio-political signifi- cance of their movement would have been in close harmony with an acclamation of Jesus as Israel's last king, the Messiah.

Another possibility comes from the idea noticed earlier in our descrip- tion of the teachings of the historical Jesus that the search for real wisdom invited people into a this-worldly spiritual "kingdom of God." As we saw earlier, near eastern movements portrayed sages as kings, because their understanding placed them in a new kind of control of their lives. After Jesus' death it would not have been too big a step to suggest that coming to see Jesus as Messiah was analogous to the successful search for wisdom that would unveil the unseen "kingdom of God spread out upon the earth." From this point of view, Jesus' followers announcing after his death that Jesus was the Messiah would have offered the same kind of tongue-in-cheek spiritual taunt that Jesus himself had used in his procla- mation of God's kingdom/empire.

So, although it is not entirely clear when and how the idea of Jesus as Messiah began, the idea that Jesus' audience or Jesus himself thought that this Galilean teacher was Israel's last king, the Messiah, could not have begun in his lifetime. Everyone understood the Messiah as a king, and everyone knew that a sage in Galilee wasn't a king.

3. The third reason that it is very difficult to think that the historical Jesus ever thought of himself as the Messiah is that the core sayings of Jesus did not show him as someone even slightly interested in his own identity. The parables are all about nature, God's domain, family interactions, other people, and commerce. The aphorisms are ingenious sayings about how life works and where to find God's domain. The gospels of Matthew, Mark, Luke, and Thomas rarely portrayed Jesus as talking about himself. In the few places where Jesus referred to himself, these gospels do not agree. What is more, the rare instances in Matthew, Mark, Luke, and Thomas where Jesus was pictured as talking about his own significance are obviously products of the gospel writers' reflections, not historical events.

Of course, the Gospel of John recorded Jesus as talking about his own significance all the time. In John Jesus turned out to be the Messiah, the Word of God at the beginning of time, the bread of life, the living water, the good shepherd, the resurrection and the life, and many other things. All of these titles Jesus gives himself in the Gospel of John. But since these sayings do not occur in any other document, and almost all of the other Jesus sayings in John have no parallels, scholars generally agree that they are not historically reliable. These sayings attributed to Jesus by the Gospel of John were rather the beliefs of the people in the community that produced this gospel.

It is difficult to conclude that Jesus thought of himself as the Messiah when according to the overwhelming preponderance of evidence he did not talk about himself at all. Of course, a sage who specialized in calling people on their pretensions in order that the domain of God might surprise them would not have been drawn in any case to promoting himself. Proclaiming yourself as the long awaited king of Israel while asking others not to call attention to themselves and to beware of conventional ways of thinking—that would have been both hypocritical and counterproductive.

Advocate for the Downtrodden?

In the Gospel of Luke Jesus was portrayed as the one anointed by God to "bring good news to the poor" and "to set free the oppressed" (4:18). In like manner, Mary, when she learns she is to give birth to Jesus, announces that this represents God having "pulled down the mighty from their thrones and exalted the lowly" (1:51). Luke portrayed Jesus not only blessing the poor, but cursing the rich (6:24). Jesus' advocacy of "the poor, and crippled, the blind, and the lame" (14:21) was Luke's regular subject matter. For every healing done by Jesus to a man, Luke had one done to a woman. Luke pictured a group of women financially supporting Jesus (8:3). In short, Luke's Jesus comes close to being a poster child for contemporary liberal Christian social activism on behalf of the impoverished, the downtrodden, and those discriminated against on the basis of gender.

Unfortunately for the promotional potential for these contemporary activist causes (all of which I personally espouse), this portrait of Jesus occurs only in the Gospel of Luke. None of the above mentioned passages in Luke have parallels in the gospels of Q, Mark, Matthew, John, or Thomas. That the vast majority of passages showing Jesus as an advocate for the poor, the oppressed, and women were unique products of Luke strongly indicates that these ideas came mostly from Luke, not from Jesus himself.

This does not necessarily mean that Jesus ignored these groups. In fact, it is relatively easy to see how this Lukan idea developed from the teachings of the historical Jesus. As outlined earlier in this chapter, it is highly probable that Jesus criticized the pretense of wealth and even of patriarchal family conventions. But Jesus' criticism of these conventional privileges seems to have sprung from his unveiling of wisdom in surprising spots. Indeed, Jesus' injunctions not to worry about food and clothing made clear that any campaign to promote the welfare of the disadvantaged in a systematic way might run the risk of missing God's subtle wisdom and surprising kingdom.

While also emphasizing the aphoristic wisdom of Jesus, two important scholars have proposed that Jesus did have a social program. John Dominic Crossan has suggested that Jesus promoted a "religious and economic egalitarianism that negated alike and at once the hierarchical and patronal normalcies of Jewish religion and Roman power" (*The Historical Jesus*, 422). This, of course, is not the Lukan liberator of women and the poor. But Crossan's picture of the historical Jesus suggests that Jesus cared deeply about the plight of some disenfranchised sectors of society.

Also agreeing that Jesus was an aphoristic sage, Marcus Borg has proposed that Jesus led a "movement."

> It was an inclusive movement, negating the boundaries of the purity system. It included women, untouchables, the poor, the maimed, and the marginalized, as well as some people of stature who found his vision attractive

... The inclusiveness of Jesus' movement embodied a radically alternative
social vision.   —*Meeting Jesus Again for the First Time*, 56

That Borg has to resort to Lukan categories for his description of the
historical Jesus may mean that he has overstated the movement dimensions of the historical Jesus' following. It is also difficult to see how Jesus
could have effected a "strategy" or "movement" from the position of a
guest speaker at other people's dinners. Both Borg and Crossan use a few
references to elaborate Jesus' questionable meal company into a social
program. Even as they admit to the historical Jesus being less an advocate
for the poor, the oppressed, and women than the Lukan Jesus, one wonders whether they may have not overstated the social program intentions
of Jesus. In any case, Crossan and Borg's portrayals of Jesus as an important social player in first-century Galilee fall well short of the idealized
social activist of Luke's gospel.

A Healer?

Twentieth-century scholarship has generally ruled out that Jesus performed what are called "nature miracles," stories of Jesus walking on the
water, calming the storm, feeding thousands of people, and raising people
from the dead, directing a miraculous catch of fish, and changing water
into wine. This conclusion still holds. The primary reasons for doubting
the historical reliability of these miracle stories are:

1. The stories themselves encourage symbolic, rather than historical,
interpretation. For instance, in Mark's discussion of the miraculous feed-
ings, Jesus chides the disciples for not understanding that the twelve baskets gathered after the feeding of the five thousand and the seven baskets
gathered after the feeding of the four thousand are secret codes for what
he was about (8:19–21). In other words, the way Mark told the stories
actually asks the reader to take the story symbolically, not at face value.

2. These nature miracles stories go against our general understanding
of what happens with storms, hungry crowds, and people who have died.
Making historical sense of ancient literature does not involve taking at
face value the talking animals of Aesop's fables, the grandiose adventures
of the Greek gods, or these nature miracle stories about Jesus.

However, other "miracle" stories about Jesus are taken much more
seriously by historians. These are the stories about Jesus as healer. The
most widely accepted "miracle" stories in terms of their historical reliability are the stories of Jesus casting out evil spirits. There are three rea-

sons why many historians think that Jesus actually did something which the gospels characterized as casting out demons:

1. There are pervasive references to such actions. Six different stories in thirteen different places in the gospels told such stories about Jesus. In addition, there are other gospel references—even as early as the pre-biblical Gospel of Q—which portrayed Jesus instructing his followers to heal in this manner.

2. Anthropology of the twentieth century has found and studied contemporary non-western cultures in which such casting out of demons benefits those who receive it. In other words, we have good scientific evidence of people healing others in ways quite similar to the gospels descriptions of Jesus' healing.

3. There is some evidence in the first-century "Christian" literature— both inside and outside the Bible—of embarrassment about the idea of Jesus healing in this way. Indeed, some of these ancient texts seem to want to discourage their readers from thinking of Jesus as a healer. For instance, the Gospel of Mark portrayed Jesus as forbidding others to speak of his casting out of demons, and the Acts of the Apostles portrayed several early "spirit" healers as harmful. This embarrassment over Jesus as healer can be seen as an indication that it was more likely to have happened.

The Jesus Seminar concluded that Jesus did such casting out of evil spirits, and both Crossan and Borg independently credit some of the stories with some historical reliability. While Robert Funk in *Honest to Jesus* is curiously silent on the matter of Jesus as this kind of healer, both Burton Mack and James Breech reject the historical reliability of these stories.

Crossan, Borg, and the Jesus Seminar as a voting constituency also credit certain other healing stories with historical reliability, including the healing of Peter's mother-in-law, the cure of someone's skin rash, the healing of a paralytic, the cure of a woman with a vaginal hemorrhage, and the causing of a blind man to see (*The Acts of Jesus*, 531).

The thorough work of John Dominic Crossan on this question of Jesus as healer is worth noting. For Crossan, Jesus' healing was not done simply as a demonstration of how powerful or caring an individual he was. Rather, Jesus' healing belonged to both his proclamation of an "unmediated" kingdom of God and the actions of his followers who were also healers. According to Crossan, "Miracle and parable, healing and eating, were calculated to force individuals into unmediated physical and spiritual contact with God and unmediated physical and spiritual contact with one another" (*The Historical Jesus*, 422).

Although—as will be noted shortly—I cannot find enough evidence to draw the same conclusions Crossan does, the way he works on the question of Jesus' miracles is worth noting as an illustration of the clear thinking in the current generation of historical Jesus studies. First of all, Crossan rules out the nature miracles for the reasons stated above. Secondly, he makes a clear tie between Jesus as healer and Jesus as sage. This is important because the great preponderance of early documentary evidence about Jesus shows him as sage. Any case for Jesus as healer must comport with Jesus as sage in order to do justice to the evidence. Thirdly, Crossan makes a strong case for Jesus' healing being a part of the social movement of people of which Jesus was a leader. For Crossan, the healing belonged to the larger message and movement.

My position on healing in the Jesus movement is slightly different from those of Crossan and the Jesus Seminar. The twentieth-century anthropological discoveries of healing in non-western societies so closely parallel the numerous stories about early Jesus people doing healing as to convince me that there were healers in the Jesus movements. The way these early movements—based in the wisdom Jesus sought and taught—enthusiastically experienced freedom from conventional bonds of family, marketplace, religion, and empire could have inspired some particularly sensitive people to heal. I do not think that Jesus was one of those healers. The anthropological studies about these healers show that they are not teachers. So, my conclusions are that the sage Jesus inspired other people in his movement to heal through his sagacious breaking open of new understanding.

In any case Jesus either performed or inspired healing in relationship to his uncovering of hidden wisdom and God's surprising domain, "spread out upon the earth." Contrary especially to the way the healing stories are told in the grandiose style of the Gospel of John, Jesus' healing or that of his followers did not call attention to the healer, and was not done to prove that Jesus was divine.

The Death of Jesus

That Jesus was crucified is one of the most solid historical assertions about him. His crucifixion was one of the only two or three pieces of information about Jesus noted by non-Christian historians of his day (the other two pieces of information from these non-Christian historians are that he taught and he had followers). Crucifixion was so shameful as a punishment that it hardly could have been invented as a story by Jesus' followers. There are far more noble ways of dying which the legend-producing early Christians would have preferred, had the knowledge of Jesus' crucifixion not been so wide-spread.

It is also very clear that Jesus was crucified by the Romans. In spite of the gospel stories of Jesus' arrest, it would have been almost impossible for Jewish leaders and people to have had a prominent role in Jesus' execution. Crucifixion was the prescribed Roman punishment for rebelling against the empire, and capital punishment was a prerogative which the Roman rulers zealously restricted to themselves and their soldiers. Both Burton Mack in *A Myth of Innocence* and John Dominic Crossan in *Who Killed Jesus?* have shown how the gospel stories of Jesus' betrayal, denial, trial before the Sanhedrin, appearance before Pilate, and burial are products of early "Christians" in their struggle against particular Jewish rivals several generations after Jesus.

Mack and Crossan disagree about the stories of Jesus' conflict with the Temple authorities shortly before his death. Mack sees these stories—which are in all four biblical gospels—as symbolic of the later tension between early Christians and the Temple, while Crossan sees them as reflecting some kind of inevitable conflict between Jesus' egalitarian movement and Temple leaders.

The largest unsettled historical question about Jesus' crucifixion is why he was crucified. The fact that all crucifixions were under Roman control presents the biggest problem, since Christian and non-Christian literature alike have no stories of direct conflict between Jesus and the Roman authorities. The explanations of Bruce Chilton and Marcus Borg that Jesus' sage-like attack on the purity systems of the Temple caused his death fall woefully short of explaining why the Roman governor executed Jesus as a rebel against Rome. Both Crossan's proposal that Jesus' "kingdom of God" teachings satirized Rome in an all-too provocative manner and Mack's proposal that Jesus' execution fit a larger pattern of Roman pacification efforts through relatively random crucifixions make more sense.

An Historical Resurrection?

The Jesus Seminar in its discussion, debate, and subsequent voting on the historicity of material about Jesus voted that his appearance to Paul in a vision after Jesus' death "is virtually certain" and "supported by a preponderance of evidence." That is the only event relative to Jesus' resurrection that the Seminar credited with historical reliability.

The subtlety of this position is worth unpacking. By validating the historical reliability of the post-crucifixion vision of Jesus by Paul, these scholars took seriously the religious experience of early followers of Jesus who experienced his presence after he died. Paul himself had written in 1 Cor 15:3, 5–8 that he had been "taught" about a number of post-crucifixion "appearances" of Jesus to different people. Indeed, such appearances could have been numerous. Greg Riley has recently suggested that such appearances of the dead were not even considered extraordinary in the Mediterranean culture of that time. Crossan follows this observation with a similar one: such appearances are also not that unusual in any culture, including our own.

Thus, crediting Paul's vision of the resurrected Jesus with historical reliability is simply saying that such visions do happen. The Seminar's votes against historical reliability for the stories of the empty tomb on "Easter" morning is the dropping of the other shoe. That is, very few historians think that the empty tomb story happened.

The reasoning for this is quite clear. First of all, the empty tomb stories seem to have been written quite late in the first century, at least two generations after Jesus died. None of the Christian literature in the first thirty years after Jesus (the Q Gospel, the Gospel of Thomas, all the letters of Paul, and the chains of miracle stories) contains empty tomb stories. The first empty tomb story is in either the biblical Gospel of Mark or in the non-biblical Gospel of Peter (there is some scholarly debate about which of these gospels was written first).

Secondly, the first literature which emphasized the resurrection, the letters of Paul, do not seem to look at resurrection historically. We have already noted the "visionary" quality of Jesus' "resurrection" for Paul. Even more striking is the way Paul seems to have included every follower of Jesus in the direct experience of the resurrection. In Rom 6:4, 11 he wrote: "When we were baptized, we went into the tomb with him and joined him in death, so that as Christ was raised from the dead by the Father's glory, we too might live a new life ... You too must consider yourselves to be dead to sin, but alive for God in Christ Jesus."

In other words, for Paul the resurrection was not an historical event which happened sometime ago in a far-off land. Rather Jesus' resurrection was something that happened when each person was baptized and when each person became "dead to sin, but alive for God." The earliest texts about the resurrection, then, were clearly dealing in symbolic discourse, not historical reporting.

Conclusion

The past two decades of historical Jesus research have profited a great deal from the new availability of the Gospel of Thomas and the Gospel of Peter. In addition, the emergence of the Q Gospel (to be discussed in more detail in chapter three), early miracle collections, all priceless evidence of the first thirty years of Jesus literature, added important data.

Although not all scholars agree, there is now a much clearer picture of the historical Jesus than existed forty years ago, when the leading German scholar on Jesus, Gunther Bornkamm, wondered whether anything could be said with much certainty about the historical Jesus. With some assurance, we can now describe Jesus as a sage living in the northern territory of Galilee who taught a surprising and subversive wisdom about God's domain. At least, he inspired healing as a part of his teaching about the way God's domain challenged family, empire, religion, and marketplace. For some reason, he was executed by the Roman empire. His followers very soon began to collect his teachings, elaborate on them, build communities in his wake, and/or experience him as a resurrected presence.

This general picture of the historical Jesus as an important Galilean sage is—even if not heroic or of mythic proportions—a rather astonishing and evocative one. Without claiming any absolute knowledge about who Jesus was, we can now posit a basic consensus that he was a noteworthy seeker of wisdom, whose teachings soon inspired many to extend his mission in a variety of ways and to form a variety of associations in his name. That this Jesus is both remarkable and limited offers a real sense of him as an historical person. This Jesus is very engaging. At the same time he is clearly not all things to all people, as the mythical and legendary Jesus of succeeding generations would become. This is a real human individual—with particularities which both limit and enhance his stature. With the possible exception of Ben Witherington's portrait of Jesus as a sage (and everything else—Messiah, hero, savior, one who walks on water), all the other major profiles of Jesus present us with someone with real historical limitations and inspiring historical achievements.

2

Layers Obscuring Jesus at Prayer

There is quite a bit of material about Jesus at prayer in the various gospels of the first one-hundred years after Jesus' death. Q, Mark, Matthew, Thomas, Luke, and John all make reference to Jesus praying. Unfortunately as we observed in the Introduction, the various portraits of Jesus at prayer do not fit together easily. Perhaps the most glaring contradiction is between the twenty-six-verse-long prayer by Jesus in chapter 17 of the Gospel of John and the instructions attributed to Jesus in Matt 6:7: "When you pray, you should not babble on as the pagans do. They imagine that the length of their prayers will command attention."

So, some sorting out of the texts about Jesus at prayer is necessary. We will need to identify which gospel references to Jesus praying are the most reliable historically. This chapter will examine a long series of texts portraying Jesus' prayer life in historically unreliable ways. These layers which obscure the historical Jesus' prayer life by promoting other agendas must be peeled back in order to obtain a clear view of some striking and reliable data about how Jesus prayed.

Fortunately most of this process of separating the historically reliable texts from others will be relatively easy. It makes most sense to start with those texts whose historical accuracy is most easily ruled out. After this chapter removes a number of layers of distracting material from the early texts, the following chapters will be able to sketch some fascinating new possibilities in the search for the historical Jesus' prayer life.

Gospel of John: Changes

The Jesus of the John's gospel—in contrast to the Jesuses of most other gospels—was portrayed as divine. This Jesus claims the divine privilege of God throughout the gospel. He utters the divine "I am" regularly, and claims to be "the way, the truth and the life," "the bread of life," "the true vine," and much else. The Johannine Jesus was never pictured as needy. In John's story, Jesus on the cross is not vulnerable at all, but rather calm-ly making sure there is someone to take care of his mother and then pro-nouncing the end with "it is finished." The very beginning of the Gospel portrayed Jesus as the Word, who in the beginning "was with God, and was God."

One wonders why this Jesus would have needed to pray at all. This question can actually be detected in the way John wrote about it. John avoided the standard Greek word for prayer (*proseuchomai*, see Box 1, p. 5) in describing Jesus talking to God in chapter 17. Furthermore in the consecutive stories of feeding the five thousand and walking on the water—found in the gospels of Mark and Matthew—Jesus was portrayed as going away to the mountain to pray between the two stories. In John's version, Jesus goes to the mountain, but does not pray. This difference probably demonstrates both that Mark, Matthew, and John depended on a common source and that John—because his Jesus was divine—removed the reference to Jesus praying.

In fact, Jesus prays only once in John's gospel. That is in the above-mentioned chapter-long prayer prior to his arrest and crucifixion. In that long prayer, Jesus speaks as a companion and partner to God, assuring God that "when I was with them, I kept them under your protection—all those you have given me, so that they may be united just as we are unit-ed." This Jesus is a cosmic companion of God and prays like one: "Father, I want those you gave into my care to be with me wherever I am, so they may see my honor—the honor you bestowed on me because you loved me before the foundations of the world." This is not the prayer of any mortal, but of a divine being talking with his divine partner and Father.

It is nearly impossible to take the seventeenth chapter of John serious-ly as an accurate representation of the way Jesus prayed. The reasons are basically two:

No other texts in the first century showed Jesus praying like this. There are no parallels to this kind of prayer by Jesus in the other docu-ments of the first hundred years. As will be shown in the rest of this chapter, no other evidence of prayer—even when obviously non-histor-ical for other reasons—portrays Jesus talking to God as a cosmic cohort as he does in the Gospel of John. In all other sources Jesus' prayer appears to be that of a human being, petitioning God for himself and others for bread, forgiveness, and support in the common ways every other human does.

The way Jesus prays in John 17 mirrors the way Jesus was portrayed in the rest of the Gospel of John (and nowhere else in the first one-hundred years). In other words, the portrait of Jesus as the divine Son and partner of God was consistent in and unique to John's gospel. Clearly then, Jesus' prayer in John 17 is a product of the author(s) of John, not of the historical Jesus.

The only other references to prayer by Jesus in the Gospel of John are consistent with this overall Johannine tendency. In both 14:16 and 16:26 John's Jesus speaks of "praying the Father" to accomplish certain things. In other words, here too the way Jesus refers to prayer cannot be historically accurate, but is a product of John's consistent and unique picture of Jesus as God's cosmic companion.

Gospel of Matthew: Additions

As we will see later in chapter 4, the Gospel of Matthew preserved some of the most historically accurate data about Jesus' prayer life. But that does not mean that everything in Matthew is accurate. In fact, it is fairly easy to identify parts of Matthew's portrait which—like those in John—are Matthew's later creations, rather than Jesus' own prayer patterns.

There are four such Matthean additions. They are so identified because they are found only in Matthew and because they show similarities to other passages found only in Matthew.

The first such picture is perhaps one of the most famous quotes attributed to Jesus about prayer: "When you pray, don't act like phonies. They love to stand up and pray in houses of worship and on street corners, so they can show off in public. I swear to you, go into a room by yourself and shut the door behind you. Then pray to your Father, the hidden one. And your Father, with his eye for the hidden, will applaud you" (6:5, 6). In other words, don't pray in public, because that leads to showing off and/or hypocrisy.

While this may be an important teaching about prayer, there is good reason to think that Matthew put it in the mouth of Jesus when Matthew wrote his gospel. The first indication of this is that this teaching is found in no other gospel: not in Mark, Luke, John, Q, or Thomas. The second is that it exhibits an attitude found in Matthew—and Matthew only—concerning other subjects. For instance, in Matt 6:1–2 we find in the mouth of Jesus the following teaching: "Take care that you don't flaunt your religion in public to be noticed by others. Otherwise, you will have no recognition from your Father in the heavens. For example, when you give to charity, don't bother to toot your own horn as some phony pietists do in houses of worship and on the street." Similarly in Matt 6:16–18— and only there—the Matthean Jesus says: "When you fast, don't make a spectacle of your remorse as the pretenders do. As you know, they make their faces unrecognizable so they may be publicly recognized. I swear to you, they have been paid in full. When you fast, comb your hair and wash your face, so your fasting may go unrecognized in public. But it will be recognized by your Father, the hidden one, and your Father, who has an eye for the hidden, will applaud you."

It is important for the overall portrait of Jesus at prayer to be developed later in this book that the well-known quote about praying in secret be recognized as a product of Matthew's attitude, not Jesus'. Later in the book there will be good reason to think of Jesus' prayer as intensely social—even to the point of the prayer itself calling for reaction by and interaction among those praying. This stands in obvious contradiction to a teaching mandating prayer in a "room by yourself."

Since one of the requirements of this book is to portray a prayer life of the historical Jesus which makes sense, the obvious contradiction of prayer in secret and intense socially interactive prayer will need to be avoided. Here I note that key to this coherent portrait of Jesus at prayer is the understanding that promoting private prayer was not a concern of the historical Jesus, but a Matthean motif.

Also from Matthew is the attitude that prayer has to do with heaven. In Matthew's version of the Lord's Prayer, "heaven" is mentioned twice whereas the Lukan and Q versions do not mention "heaven" at all. The "who art in heaven" part of the Lord's Prayer is clearly a Matthean addition, as is "enact your will on earth as you have in heaven." This does not necessarily mean that the historical Jesus would not have thought he was praying to God in heaven. It simply indicates there is no evidence either way whether Jesus directed his prayer "to heaven."

But clearly Matthew linked prayer and heaven. This is typical of an overall interest by Matthew in heaven, which did not seem to be shared by Mark, Luke, John, Thomas, or the historical Jesus. For instance, Matthew used the word "heaven" seventy-six times in his gospel, whereas Mark used it only fourteen times and Luke only twenty-four times.

A third Matthean addition not shared by the historical Jesus concerns evil. Only in Matthew does Jesus pray: "Deliver us from evil." This is also typical of Matthew, who in his gospel mentioned evil twenty-four times, in contrast to the five times Mark did and the eleven times Luke did. This probably reflects Matthew's more intense focus on moral issues than we find in any of the other gospels.

The fourth Matthean addition to the theme of prayer was his association of prayer with fasting. As noted above, the instructions about unostentatious prayer employed almost the same words as the instruction on unobtrusive fasting. Similarly in some manuscripts of Matt 17:20, 21—and nowhere else—Jesus says: "If you have faith as a grain of mustard seed, you will say to this mountain, 'Move from here to there,' and it will move; and nothing will be impossible to you. But this kind never comes out except by prayer and fasting." These combinations of prayer and fasting are all the more noteworthy in Matthew because in Mark, Thomas, and Luke Jesus tells his followers that they do not need to fast. In other words, only according to Matthew is prayer to be accompanied by fasting. There is no evidence elsewhere that the historical Jesus recommended prayer with fasting.

Gospel of Luke: Much Prayer

It was Luke who made Jesus into a person who prays a great deal. None of the gospels except Luke attest to the frequency of Jesus' prayer. Matthew, Mark, and Luke all have Jesus praying in Gethsemane before his arrest. Each of them have Jesus praying something—although in each case, something very different—from the cross. And, Matthew and Luke portrayed Jesus praying at least a portion of that which eventually became the Lord's Prayer. But in Matthew and Mark Jesus prays only one other time (the aforementioned juncture between the feeding of the five thousand and the walking on water).

But in the Gospel of Luke Jesus prays a great deal. For instance, only Luke portrayed Jesus praying at his own baptism (3:21). Only in Luke do we read that right before Jesus called the disciples and selected the twelve that "he went to the mountain to pray, and spent the night in prayer to God" (6:12). At a similarly crucial moment in the story of Peter's confession that Matthew, Mark, and Luke share, only Luke wrote that Jesus was praying right before Peter spoke (9:18). In the same vein, only Luke's story of Jesus being transfigured on the mountain contained the assertion that it happened "as he was praying" (9:29). Only in Luke does Jesus begin to teach his disciples to pray, after he himself was "praying in a certain place" (11:1). The parable about the different ways the Pharisee and the toll collector prayed in the Temple is only in Luke (18:10–14). And Luke's gospel was the only one to instruct people to pray in a time of crisis: "Pray constantly that you may have the strength to escape all these things that are about to occur ..." (21:36).

All these examples of Luke inserting prayer into the story-line of Jesus cannot be accidental. Clearly, Luke wanted to portray Jesus as one who prayed a great deal. Nor can it be accidental that the Lukan Jesus always devotes himself to prayer at crucial moments in the story (e.g. the baptism, the calling of the disciples, the confession that he is Messiah, and the transfiguration). Luke meant to show Jesus and his followers turning to prayer in times of crisis. Since Luke was written later than Mark (and perhaps Matthew), it is clear that Luke revised the previous pictures of Jesus in order to make him into someone dedicated to prayer.

In Luke Jesus goes off alone to pray—a practice he observes less often in Mark and Matthew (and not at all in John). The Lukan inclusion of prayer in describing the baptism and the choosing of the disciples has already been noted. In addition, Luke 5:16 has Jesus withdrawing into the wilderness to pray in a story in which Mark and Matthew made no mention of prayer. Jesus' withdrawal for prayer happens twice in Mark and and once in Matthew, but between three and six times in Luke—depending on how the texts are read.

This raises a pointed question about the conventional picture of Jesus retreating for prayer into a place where he is alone. Since this kind of praying was primarily a Lukan motif, it is important to ask whether the historical Jesus did much of this kind of prayer. This question gains additional significance when we remember that the instructions to pray in secret were almost certainly from Matthew, not from the historical Jesus (cf. above review of special attitudes about prayer in Matthew). Finally, questioning how much Jesus did this kind of prayer in retreat will be raised by the new style of prayer by the historical Jesus described later in the next three chapters. This new style of prayer—based on strong textual evidence to be addressed in the next chapter—was most likely intensely socially interactive prayer by the historical Jesus. There is obviously a degree of contradiction between a Jesus who always retreated to pray and a Jesus who thrived on group prayer.

It is important to clarify here that we can much more easily trace the differences among Luke, Matthew, Mark, and John, since they all are still available as written sources. Less clear are the differences between Luke's stories of the prayerful Jesus and the historical Jesus himself. That Luke's Jesus at prayer was a product of the Lukan imagination is clear. That many Lukan scenes of Jesus at prayer were imagined by Luke is also clear, since so many of them portray Jesus alone at prayer. (Who could have reported that Jesus prayed, if he was alone?) Luke's picture of Jesus at prayer was largely due to his own understanding of prayer, and therefore does not offer reliable information about the historical Jesus. We will have to wait for a more complete sorting of the data, as this chapter and the next unfold, before concluding how much or how little the historical Jesus prayed.

Gospel of Mark: Little Prayer

If one depended on the Gospel of Mark for an understanding of Jesus' prayer life, there would be little to go on. Based on Mark, one would con-clude that Jesus did not pray much. This is all the more curious, since Mark was the first biblical gospel written. It should be noted, however, that some scholars now think that the Gospel of Thomas, which is not in the Christian Bible, was written before Mark; and most scholars propose that the Q Gospel, the re-constructed source of sayings for Matthew and Luke (discussed at length in the next chapter), was written before Mark.

Perhaps the most attention given to the question of Jesus at prayer in the Gospel of Mark is the scene of Jesus praying in the Garden of Gethsemane before his arrest. Most scholars think that this story origi-nates with Mark. The story seems to have two purposes: one relates to prayer and the other does not.

The Gethsemane story tells of Jesus at prayer after a last supper and before his arrest. He is pictured as having brought disciples with him to Gethsemane; taken Peter, James, and John with him a little farther, and then—asking the three to be watchful—gone yet a little farther alone to pray. His prayer addressed to his "Abba, Father" is that this cup (his pas-sion and death) might be "removed" from him. He returns three times to Peter, James, and John, each time finding them asleep.

Much of this story reflects a major theme in the rest of Mark's gospel: the failure of Peter, James, and John to understand what it really meant to follow Jesus. Mark was the composer of the stories about Peter being called "Satan" by Jesus (8:33), Peter denying Jesus three times (14:26–31, 66–72), and the disciples not understanding the parables Jesus taught (4:10–13). So the threefold failure of Peter, James, and John to watch for Jesus while he prayed was part of a larger Markan portrait of these disci-ples. This anti-Peter attitude by Mark most likely came from the commu-nity of Mark which apparently felt betrayed by Peter and James' position that everyone who followed Jesus needed to be circumcised (Gal 2:6–13). So, from the point of view of historical accuracy, Mark's portrayal of Jesus, Peter, and James cannot be taken at face value.

The other part of the Gethsemane story shows Jesus at prayer in a

desperate situation. He pleads to God to release him from the coming suffering and death. This strikingly vulnerable prayer with Jesus saying his
"soul is very sorrowful, even to death," portrayed a Jesus who prayed his
weakness and sorrow to God. This picture of an agonized Jesus made the
writers of Luke and John so nervous that they either softened or dropped
this scene completely. This despairing prayer was paralleled in Mark's portrait of Jesus on the cross in which Jesus' only statement is "My God, my
God, why have you abandoned me" (Mark 15:34)?

There can be little doubt that Jesus' Gethsemane prayer in Mark (or
Matthew or John) was fictional. After all, Mark tells us Jesus was alone.
So from the story itself, we know that there was no one with Jesus to hear
what he said. The words of Jesus' Gethsemane prayer in Mark must have
been the product of Mark's imagination.

It may be less clear, however, that the Markan Jesus' words: "Take this
cup from me..." communicate something important about the historical
Jesus' prayer life, even if the words themselves are fictional. They so clearly match the spirit of the agonized cry from the cross in Mark as to pose
interesting questions about Jesus' prayer life:

- Did Jesus cry out in doubt to God during his passion and crucifixion?

Since we have already noted the almost certain fiction of his prayer in
Gethsemane, the crucial question hinges on the cry from the cross. Its
historicity can be gauged with considerable accuracy since the phrase,
like a number of elements of Mark's passion story come from Psalm 22.
For instance, the dividing of Jesus' clothes and the casting of lots for them
comes directly from Ps 22:18, as does the wagging of heads in derision
(22:7). In other words, Mark seems to have taken phrases from the dis-
tressed debtor who is praying to God for relief in Psalm 22 and made them
into elements of the story of Jesus on the cross. This was a fairly common
device of story-telling in Judaism and other cultures of the Mediterranean
world of the first century. This also then seems to account for the use of
"My God, my God, why have you abandoned me?" in the Markan Jesus'
mouth. Mark placed that in Jesus' mouth, not because it was historically
accurate, but because he was using Psalm 22 to compose a story about
Jesus' death.

- Was the gut-wrenching prayer of despair found in this portrayal of
  Jesus' passion and death something that Jesus would have done?

On the positive side of the ledger, the finely drawn humanity of Jesus
in pain and doubt has a good deal of historical plausibility. Similarly, we

know from the psalmists and the prophets that Jews did not hesitate to speak their agony and doubts in prayer. On the other hand, since so much of Mark's account of Jesus' passion is clearly fictionalized, there is little reason to trust his account as historically reliable. The best that can be said is that Mark's Gethsemane and crucifixion prayers seem like something that a Jew in great pain at that time might have said in those circumstances.

Except at Gethsemane Jesus prays very little in Mark. In addition to the passage already cited from Mark 6, only one reference to Jesus praying appears in the first chapter when Mark tells of Jesus withdrawing into a lonely place to pray after Simon's mother-in-law was healed.

In no other passages in Mark does Jesus pray at all. It is quite telling that Mark does not even include Jesus teaching prayer. There is no version of the Lord's Prayer in Mark. In the next chapter parts of the Lord's Prayer will become important primary data about the historical Jesus' prayer life, but even that prayer fails to appear in this earliest of the Bible's gospels.

Gospel of Thomas: Mystical Prayer?

Many scholars now think that the Gospel of Thomas contains important material for understanding who the historical Jesus was. The case for Jesus as sage made by so many scholars and summarized in chapter 1 rests to a certain degree on the discovery of the Gospel of Thomas, which contains only sage-like sayings of Jesus. Unfortunately, the discussion of prayer in the Gospel of Thomas does not seem to be a reliable indicator of how the historical Jesus prayed.

Prayer as such is not mentioned in a positive light in the Gospel of Thomas. The only two relevant texts are somewhat dismissive of prayer. In Thom 14:1–5 Jesus says: "If you fast, you will bring sin upon yourselves, and if you pray, you will be condemned, and if you give to charity, you will harm your spirits. When you go into any region and walk about in the countryside, when people take you in, eat what they serve you and heal the sick among them. After all, what goes into your mouth will not defile you; rather it is what comes out of your mouth that will defile you."

In this passage Thomas was re-positioning Jesus over against three basics of Judean religious practice: fasting, prayer, and acts of loving-kindness. Thomas went so far as to re-shape the saying about what defiles a person to make it a saying against prayer. This saying in Mark 7:15 attacks religious prescriptions about what you can or cannot eat. Probably originating from Jesus himself, this Markan saying contrasted what went into a person—food, which is not dirty—and what came out of a person —defecation, which is dirty. Thomas has re-worked this saying to con-trast what goes into and comes out of a person's mouth, in order to posi-tion Jesus over against the traditional piety of fasting, prayer, and loving-kindness.

A similarly antagonistic Thomas saying is found in 104:1, 2: "They said to Jesus, 'come let us pray today, and let us fast.' Jesus said, 'What sin have I committed, or how have I been undone. Rather, when the groom leaves the bridal suite, then let the people fast and pray.'" Here also Thomas combined prayer and fasting, and did not recommend them. Indeed, the text seems to have rejected explicitly that Jesus prayed at all.

The passage did leave open the possibility of people praying after Jesus was no longer with them. That his followers developed a new toward prayer may be evidenced in a series of passages in Thomas in which Jesus holds up "the two becoming one" as important. For instance, in 61:5, Jesus says: "If one is whole, one will be filled with light, but if one is divid-ed, one will be filled will darkness." And, in 22:5a, 7 he has portrayed Jesus as saying, "When you make the two into one, ... then you will enter the Father's domain." This emphasis on the spiritual virtue of the two becoming one has clear prayer implications in 106:1, 2 where Jesus says: "When you make the two into one, you will become children of Adam, and when you say, 'Mountain, move from here, it will move.'" The say-ing about moving a mountain—to be discussed later in this chapter—was associated with the power of prayer in Mark and Matthew. It is plausible, then, that the two becoming one (also mentioned in Thomas 11, 30, and 48) was a Thomasine image of mystical union in prayer which gave great powers to Jesus' followers after Jesus was no longer with them.

But all of this reflection on prayer and fasting by Jesus in Thomas must be considered historically inaccurate, on account of difficulties similar to those encountered in John's discussion of Jesus at prayer. Neither the material in Thomas nor John is found in any other first century texts. For this reason the ways Jesus prays in both these gospels must be considered a creation of the writer, not of Jesus himself.

Jesus Prays on the Cross

In this survey of prayer material in the gospels we have glossed over some of the most explicit and dramatic prayers of Jesus, those uttered on the cross. Matthew, Mark, and Luke all pictured Jesus praying while he died. John—in complete agreement with his portrayal of Jesus as a divine and cosmic figure—did not show Jesus praying on the cross. For John the cross was not a problem for Jesus, but rather his "hour of glory."

But the crucifixion prayers in Matthew, Mark, and Luke need to be a part of our examination. When studied closely, they end up being rather perfect examples of prayer material produced by each particular gospel writer, and as such must be peeled away as historically unreliable.

In this chapter's section on Markan prayer material, we noted the parallel between prayers of agony in Gethsemane and protest from the cross. Having recognized the crucifixion prayer as a quote from Psalm 22 and hence not a historically accurate report, that section also noted the tangible humanity of Jesus on the cross. This human quality offered, if not an accurate record of prayer, at least, some implicit historical perspective. It needs to be added, however, that Jesus' agony in prayer on the cross suits well with another major Markan theme. Throughout Mark's gospel, the suffering and seemingly non-triumphant character of Jesus was emphasized. It is worth remembering that the original ending to the gospel of Mark presented a very ambiguous "resurrection" scene.

The women discover the empty tomb, run away frightened, and tell no one. That is the end of Mark's gospel. In a similar vein, Peter is chastised after having proclaimed Jesus the Messiah and is told that everyone who follows Jesus must pick up a cross as well. That is, the Markan Jesus' prayer on the cross fits completely with the Markan story of a suffering, non-triumphant Jesus.

Matthew's picture of Jesus at prayer on the cross followed Mark exactly, illustrating clearly that he (like Luke) has copied a good deal of Mark's story. Jesus' only prayer—indeed as in Mark his only words—is "My God, my God, why have you abandoned me?"

But this picture of Jesus in agonizing prayer was too stark for Luke. As we remember from the survey of Luke, his Jesus prays often and finds solace in prayer. So Luke changed Mark's words completely. Having prayed at all the other important junctures of his life, Luke's Jesus must pray on the cross. But the prayer must reflect the peace the Lukan Jesus found in prayer. So instead of the abandonment prayer, Luke's Jesus on the cross prays, "Father, into your hands I commit my spirit." That Luke changed Mark and that the change reflected Luke's general attitude about Jesus at prayer make it clear that this prayer was not from the historical Jesus, but from Luke.

Moving Mountains and the Mustard Seed

One other small set of Jesus prayer materials alluded to in the discussion of the Gospel of Thomas now requires a bit more attention to determine whether the sayings go back to the historical Jesus. Five sayings attributed to Jesus in Mark, Matthew, and Thomas present Jesus telling his followers that if they tell a mountain to move, it will move.

Two different versions of this saying appear in Thomas 48 and 106. Each associates 'making peace' or 'becoming one' with the ability to move mountains. In the review of Thomas we suggested that such vocabulary could reflect a special kind of mystical prayer in the Thomas community, but that the teaching itself is not traceable to Jesus because of the special Thomasine vocabulary (the two and the one).

A similar saying occurs in both Mark (11:20–25) and Matthew (21:18–22). As in the crucifixion prayers Matthew basically followed Mark, so also in the following three-part sequence: (1) Jesus curses a fig tree, and his followers express astonishment that the fig tree has withered because of Jesus' curse. (2) Jesus replies: "Those who say to this mountain, 'Up with you and into the sea!' and do not waver in their conviction, but trust what they say will happen, that's the way it will be." (3) Jesus adds: "This is why I keep telling you, trust that you will receive everything you pray and ask for, and that's the way it will turn out" (Mark 11:22–24).

Close attention to this story reveals that the connections between the three parts of the story are quite loose—indeed almost disjointed. The connections between (1) and (2) are fairly logical, and the point is that just as Jesus had the power to wither the fig tree, his followers have the power to move mountains. The connections between (2) and (3) are less strong. They would be stronger if their order were reversed, so that the logic would be: You will receive anything you pray or ask for, so you could successfully pray to have a mountain cast into the sea. The formulation of (3) seems to be aware of the clumsy order, and tries to include (1), (2), and (3)—albeit rather clumsily—by combining the "praying" and "asking for" actions. Finally, there seems to be really no connection between (1) and (3). So it is not at all clear how this saying came to be. It appears to have been patched together.

Such is also the impression made by the final saying in this curious set. This saying found in Matthew does not follow anything in Mark: "Even if you have trust no larger than a mustard seed, you will say to this mountain, 'Move from here to there,' and it will move. And nothing will be beyond you" (17:20). Here the saying about moving mountains seems to have been mixed with the parable comparing the reign of God to the way a mustard seed grows. In this version of the saying, Matthew did not have Jesus mention prayer at all. Separating the mountain moving from the prayer context seems to confirm the sense we get from the Matthew 21 text that the mountain moving may indeed be somewhat superficially associated with prayer.

In this perhaps the most complicated exercise of peeling back prayer material related to Jesus, it seems that some saying about moving mountains might have gone back to Jesus himself. It is much less clear that such a saying would necessarily have been about prayer. It could just as likely have meant something like another teaching of Jesus: "Ask—it will be given to you; seek—you'll find; knock it'll be opened for you" (Matt 7:7; Luke 11:9; Thom 2:1; Thom 92;1). This ask/seek/knock saying, which like the mountain saying eventually became associated with prayer, seems to have not been associated with prayer in Jesus' mind. As Robert Funk has pointed out, the teaching about ask/seek/knock fits best with the lifestyle of Jesus and his followers who cast themselves on God's care by going from village to village, knocking on doors to see if anyone would shelter and feed them (*Honest to Jesus*, 212). It is clear that fairly early after Jesus' death such a saying about moving a mountain started being freely associated with other material (e.g. the fig tree cursing, the mustard seed parable, and prayer) in order to make more sense of it. Seen in this way then, we would have to say that if some 'you can move mountains' saying went back to Jesus, its initial meaning was probably not about prayer.

A Provisional Negative Assessment of the Material So Far

We have sorted through a massive amount of material in the gospels of the first century. This survey has been able to identify a good deal of material about Jesus and prayer, which is the product of the particular gospel writers. We have seen how particular—and in some cases peculiar—styles and viewpoints of the gospel writers about prayer have shaped each gospel's portrait of Jesus at prayer. The consistency with which the writers have pursued their own vision of Jesus at prayer has made it rather easy to conclude that much of what they have written was neither historically accurate nor even intended to be. Everything from John's divine Son Jesus in inimitable union with the Father, to Luke's cameos of Jesus at prayer at pivotal moments in the story, to Matthew and Thomas' linking of fasting and prayer—all these have clearly shown the fingerprints of the particular gospel writer clearly on the image of Jesus at prayer.

Another way of summarizing the material covered so far would be to repeat the remarks of this book's Introduction. There it was noted that when these various gospel portraits of Jesus praying are set beside each other, the composite portrait is somewhere between comical and bizarre. The agonizing crucifixion prayer of Jesus in Mark has nothing in common with the cosmic and kingly prayer of Jesus in John. The ever-prayerful Lukan Jesus stands in complete opposition to the Jesus of Thomas, who apparently rejects prayer altogether.

In the face of the powerful and creative fictions of the respective gospel writers, I want to comment that although the gospel writers' portrayals of Jesus at prayer did not serve the cause of historical accuracy well, that in itself is not reason to dismiss the value of their portraits of Jesus at prayer. They simply have another kind of value. Most scriptural scholars agree that the gospel writers did not even want to be historically accurate. Rather, the gospels were written, as the Gospel of John puts it in 20:31 "so that you will come to believe." In other words, these gospel portraits of Jesus at prayer were not written primarily to describe how Jesus prayed. They aimed at helping people learn how to pray in their own circumstances. The portraits of Jesus at prayer in each of the gospels were different, because each was fostering a particular spirituality in a unique setting.

And, of course, one cannot absolutely claim that a particular gospel writer's emphasis—whether it be the divine monologue of Jesus in John or the prayer at every crossroads policy of Luke's Jesus—is historically false. We simply note that when material is presented by only one gospel writer, and in a way consistent with that writer's overall point of view, the material is much less likely to be historically accurate.

But our quest in this book is focused on the historical Jesus, and how he prayed. To discover that, we do need some good historical data. Happily, what we have examined so far does not exhaust the available resources. There is another level of material about Jesus at prayer which contains early material bearing fewer of the fingerprints and eraser marks of the gospel writers. This material comes mostly from the Q Gospel, which was incorporated into both the Gospels of Matthew and Luke. This material also promises to be astonishingly consistent with the portrait of Jesus as sage emerging in the scholarship of our day.

3

The Q Prayer

CLOSER TO THE CORE

After seeing how the early Christian gospel writers assertively re-cast their pictures of Jesus at prayer for their own purposes, one could easily wonder whether any prayer material from Jesus himself could have survived. As we have seen, most of the gospel material about Jesus at prayer leads us astray from an historically reliable picture.

One group of Galilean sages living a generation after Jesus, managed almost by accident to preserve very valuable prayer material related to the historical Jesus. That group has come in the twentieth century to be called the Q movement, named after the document they produced in their own search for wisdom following Jesus' model. This chapter tells the story of their prayer life and how it brings us several steps closer to how Jesus prayed. By and large, what follows is based on two relatively recent works: *The Formation of Q* by John Kloppenborg and *Q: The Lost Gospel* by Burton L. Mack. Although neither Kloppenborg nor Mack have focused on prayers in Q, their breakthroughs in Q research form the foundations for this chapter's discovery of some reliable traces of Jesus' own prayer.

The Q People

Living in and near the same villages where Jesus did, there came to be a loosely knit group of Galileans who after his death continued to pursue his search for wisdom. Some of them were wandering sages, who, after the manner of Jesus might travel one or two days and walk away from their home village in their search for wisdom. Some of them were also householders, hosting meals in their own villages for the curious and the wandering sages. For the most part, this loose set of associated people were

49

enlivened by and devoted to who they had become when Jesus was still among them. Some of them were probably able to heal some sick people as an expression of this enlivened sense of wisdom uncovered and an emerging rule of God.

These Q people continued the critique of the conventions of family, wealth, empire, and religion, that had started with Jesus. They continued to experience the uncovering of new wisdom and the arrival of a new "basileia" as they risked freeing themselves from these old conventions. With their loose alliance between householders and wanderers, they were able to continue both the wandering style of the sage and the meal occa-sions for learning together. When they came together, they created more of their own aphorisms and challenges to convention. They recalled Jesus' own teachings, partly as a way to keep the energies flowing and partly as a sign of allegiance.

In the villages where they lived and visited the Q people pursued their agenda of criticizing basic conventions of life for several decades (in con-trast to the short time Jesus was so engaged). As a result, they had a fair-ly large number of opponents. Certainly within the first fifteen years after Jesus' death, there were many occasions on which these Q sages would be turned away from someone's village banquet for unpopular criticisms made on previous visits. Many of the wealthy became angry at the way the Q people flaunted their lack of dependence on possessions. A grow-ing number of families were outraged by having a family member join the Q group and then criticize the long-held values of family loyalty, control, and dependence. The synagogues, made nervous by the group's critique of religious conventions, became reactive and resistant to the Q people. Interestingly enough, it appears that the Roman imperial government was the only institution criticized by Q which did not worry about Q's cri-tique, considering them too small a movement to bother with.

But by the year 50 the Q movement in Galilee was embattled. To be sure, they were still attracting people to their experience of the new "basileia" and to their confident search that all wisdom would be uncov-ered and all sham would be exposed. But there were now whole villages where they were not welcome. A number of Q adherents had been called before their synagogues' authorities to examine whether they should be allowed to continue associating with the synagogue. By 60 C.E. there were probably some synagogues who had expelled Q people. Certainly by then there were networks of wealthy people in active opposition to the new Q wisdom, and countless families deeply resentful of Q people who were undermining their long traditions of allegiance.

The Q People Fight Back

Between the years 40 and 65, the Q movement developed a series of strategies to respond to increasing antagonism in the villages of Galilee. These strategies were:

1. They started writing their wisdom down. The short inspiring and challenging sayings of Jesus and their own, which kept them focused on why they were committed to this lifestyle and search for wisdom, were collected in written form. It is this writing, recovered only by scholars in the last eighty years, which has let us know that there was such a movement in Galilee in the 40s–60s (see Box 3, p. 16).

2. They began to claim Jesus as their founder. As they were challenged from various sides as to what grounds they had for their critique, the Q people came increasingly to rely on the idea that they had a great teacher at the beginning of their movement. Particularly in their debates with the synagogues, who wanted to know how the Q movement as a Jewish movement could justify its critique of family and religious traditions, the Q people increasingly spoke in the name of their founder Jesus. They did this in two ways: a) when the synagogue authorities asked them to quote from the Hebrew scriptures to justify themselves, the Q people instead quoted from Jesus; and b) the Q people portrayed Jesus as "one of the prophets" who had been rejected so often by God's people in the past.

3. They began to compose and write down increasingly angry sayings, condemning those who rejected them. These sayings—all in the name of Jesus—often focused on a predicted cataclysmic end to the world in which their opponents would be punished. For instance, in Q 10:14,15, the anger overflowed: "Tyre and Sidon will be better off at the judgment than you. And you, Capernaum, you don't think you'll be exalted in heaven, do you? No, you'll go to Hell." John Kloppenborg's book mentioned above shows how the Q document is layered in its composition, and how the second layer of material was all apocalyptically angry.

4. They began to institutionalize prayer as a response to their situation. The more they were alienated from the synagogue prayer service—both by their own critique and the reaction to it—the more they needed their own prayer traditions. The more organized and embattled from the outside their meal gatherings became, the more they needed to have a stable sense of God with them. In keeping with their other strategies of response, they needed a prayer that would root them in their connection to Jesus. This, of course, is our primary interest in Q.

Q's Jesus Prayer

So as a way of coping with their embattled position, the Q movement composed a prayer. Like many Jewish prayers of that day, it was a prayer to be repeated. It was a Jesus prayer. That is, it was a prayer in which they claimed their connection to Jesus. Just as they heard Jesus in all the sayings they wrote down, they heard Jesus in this prayer which they memorized, repeated, and wrote down.

In composing the prayer, they drew on several important resources: (1) some synagogue prayer; (2) some prayer material from Jesus, as near as they could remember it; and most importantly, (3) words that reminded them of who they were and helped them in their increasingly entrenched positions.

The prayer went something like this:

> Abba/Father,
> Your name be revered.
> Let your basileia/kingdom/reign come.
> Give us the bread we need for today
> And forgive us our debts to the extent that we forgive those
> who are in debt to us.
> And please don't subject us to test after test.

The prayer was a brilliant source of strength for the Q people. It kept them focused on their risk-filled journey ("give us the bread we need for today"). It contained deep self-critique ("forgive us our debts only inasmuch as we do the same"). It flew the flag of the new basileia ("let you reign come"). It pleaded that the opposition not be too much ("please don't subject us to test after test"). And, as we will see later, it kept them very much in touch with the fresh, aphoristic wit of Jesus.

The way that Q's strategic prayer of resistance ended up preserving key elements of Jesus' own prayer life is the subject of the next chapter. Before we proceed to that, three side-bar questions need to be addressed by virtue of the material covered in this chapter. These three questions are:

1. What exactly is the Q document and how do we know about it?
2. The Q Jesus prayer sounds very much like the Lord's Prayer. How is the Q Jesus prayer different and how did the Lord's Prayer come into existence?
3. How do we know that the Q Jesus prayer did not originate with the historical Jesus himself rather than the Q movement?

The Q Document

In the late 1800s and early 1900s a number of German biblical schol-ars pursued a set of curious phenomena that they had observed in the gospels of Matthew, Mark, and Luke. They noticed that these three gospels—but not John—had essentially the same story line. But Matthew and Luke both had some 240 verses of teachings by Jesus that Mark did not. These teachings were very similar in Matthew and Luke, but they were located at different points Matthew and Luke's stories. For instance, the four beatitudes about the blessedness of the poor, the hungry, the weeping, and the persecuted were in both Matthew and Luke. They appeared as a part of an extended "sermon on the mount" in Matthew, but as a part of a much shorter speech on a plain in Luke.

In the early 1900s a theory arose among those German scholars to explain these curiosities. They proposed that Mark was the first gospel, and that Matthew and Luke followed Mark's story line, with some excep-tions. (This theory has in the meantime proved to be almost completely accurate.)

They also suggested that both Matthew and Luke possessed another source (the German word for source is "Quelle") which was simply a long collection of the teachings of Jesus. According to this theory the 240 verses of teaching which both Matthew and Luke contained, but in dif-ferent places in the story, come from this source. Both Matthew and Luke, according to this theory, took the sayings of the source/Quelle and put them into "Mark's story" in different places. Instead of always saying the word "source" or "Quelle", the German scholars fairly quickly short-ened the name of this hypothetical document to "Q."

Soon, however, this theory came under scrutiny and criticism. Upon isolating these some 240 sayings, one noticed two problems: (1) Such a document had no story line. Such a Q document would have been slop-py and boring, this criticism said, since it had no story line; and (2) None of the sayings in this hypothetical Q referred to Jesus' passion of Jesus and his resurrection. How could such an early Christian document fail to pre-sent Jesus—if only in legendary form—speaking of his own death and res-urrection as he does in the Gospel of Mark? These two very important criticisms made many scholars doubt the Q hypothesis for much of the twentieth century.

These doubts disappeared in a fairly dramatic fashion due to a major document discovery. In 1945 a jar of documents was found in the

Egyptian desert near the town of Nag Hammadi. Among other things this jar contained the first complete text of the Gospel of Thomas (fragments had been known beforehand and others have been discovered since). The gospel, although clearly a complete document, contained only sayings attributed to Jesus (no story line), and none of them contained any mention of the passion or resurrection of Jesus.

The Gospel of Thomas is not the Q document. The two do contain many of the same teachings of Jesus. As we have seen earlier, this overlapping of the sayings has helped historical Jesus research enormously in refining the picture of Jesus. But for Q research, the crucial importance of Thomas was that it proved that a document could be comprised only of sayings of Jesus, none of which mention his passion or resurrection. Since the discovery of Thomas, most scripture scholars have dropped their doubts about the existence of a Q document.

This has focused new attention on Q. Kloppenborg's and Mack's books, on which this chapter depends, are perhaps the leading examples of this interest. This scholarly research has afforded us considerable knowledge of the Q movement in Galilee in the 40s through the 60s. It is, of course, the document Q which contains the Q Jesus prayer, which will be so critical in our continued search for the prayer life of the historical Jesus.

The Q Prayer and the Lord's Prayer

The Lord's Prayer or Our Father is not found in any gospel. Few church-going Christians realize that the prayer "Jesus taught us," as countless liturgies say, does not exist in any part of the Bible. As we have noted earlier, in Mark and John Jesus does not teach prayer at all. Both Matthew and Luke have Jesus teaching a prayer that resembles the Lord's Prayer, but it is not the prayer people say in church. Furthermore, the prayer is substantially different in Luke and Matthew.

Both Luke and Matthew inherited the Jesus Prayer from Q, and changed it to suit their own purposes. One can easily see both Luke's and Matthew's editorial styles at work. Luke changed some of the wording to make it more comprehensible to gentiles, but did not add additional phrases. Matthew, while staying closer to the Jewish phrases in Q, felt free to add other material to the prayer.

The so-called Lord's Prayer is found in nearly complete form for the first time in another first century document, the Didache, which was not included in the New Testament (see Box 4). The Didache version included everything in the eventual Lord's Prayer but the "kingdom" part of the last line ("for yours is the kingdom and power and glory forever"), which was not included at all in Matthew and Luke. It appears that the Didache borrowed Matthew's expanded version of the Q prayer, and added further material. Basically then the Lord's Prayer said in churches in our day came into existence in four phases: Q, Matthew, the Didache, and the adding of the final word "kingdom" by several third-century documents.

Origins of the Q Prayer

Since there is no document earlier than Q, one might wonder why it might not be a reliable source for Jesus' prayer words. The answer, as shown earlier, is that this Jesus Prayer makes a great deal more sense as a

---

Box 4: Five Different Jesus Prayers of Early Christianity

The Q Gospel

"Abba/Father,
Your name be revered.
Let your basileia/kingdom/reign come.
Give us the bread we need for today
And forgive us our debts to the extent that we forgive those who
are in debt to us.
And please don't subject us to test after test."

Matthew:	Luke:
Our Father in the heavens,	Father,
your name be revered.	your name be revered.
Let your kingdom come.	Let your kingdom come.
Enact your will on earth	
as you have in heaven.	
Give us the bread.	Give us the bread
we need for today.	we need day by day.
Forgive our debts.	Forgive our sins,
to the extent we have forgiven	since we too forgive
those in debt to us.	everyone in debt to us.
And please don't subject us	And please don't subject us
to test after test,	to test after test.
but rescue us from the evil one.	

The Didache (and the ancient prayer
closest to that prayed in most Roman Catholic settings)
> Our Father
> in the heavens,
> your name be revered.
> Let your kingdom come.
> Enact your will on earth
> as you have in heaven.
> Give us the bread
> we need for today.
> Forgive our debts
> to the extent we have forgiven
> those in debt to us.
> And please don't subject us
> to test after test,
> but rescue us from the evil one,
> for yours is the power and glory forever.

Several later manuscripts (and the ancient prayer
closest to that prayed in most Protestant settings)
> Our Father
> in the heavens,
> your name be revered.
> Let your kingdom come.
> Enact your will on earth
> as you have in heaven.
> Give us the bread
> we need for today.
> Forgive our debts
> to the extent we have forgiven
> those in debt to us.
> And please don't subject us
> to test after test,
> but rescue us from the evil one,
> for yours is the kingdom and power and glory forever.

composition of the Q community. Anyone wishing to assign it as an entirety to Jesus needs to examine the following four reasons for situating its creation with Q rather than with Jesus himself:

1. As outlined above, the prayer itself fits the life situation of the Q community very well. It represents a subtle combination of traditional

Jewish prayer, embattled self-consciousness of the group under fire, and reminders of their founder.

2. There are examples from the first century of other early "Christian" groups composing prayers from various loose strands of sentence prayers. In both Luke 1:46–55 and 1:67–79 and Revelation 4 and 5 we find prayers which have been constructed from smaller units and made into a new whole, just as Q seems to have constructed its Jesus prayer from a variety of previously existing Jewish prayers and Jesus' words. So there are other examples of later communities composing prayers in this way.

3. The prayer itself is quite highly structured. It is thematically organized, moving from talking about God to talking about humans. Its rhythms, both in the Greek we find in the Q text and the Aramaic that the Q people and Jesus spoke, reflect fairly formal poetic and liturgical parallelisms. This signifies that the prayer was meant for more formal settings than any of the gospels put Jesus in. Not even the later gospels of Luke and John pictured Jesus teaching prayer in a formal setting like a synagogue or standard household situations.

4. Jesus' aphoristic style of teaching generally tried to subvert convention, not create or support it. His teachings challenged the assumptions of religion and culture, and encouraged listeners to draw on the resources they had within themselves. It is difficult to see this kind of unconventional sage teaching others to memorize a prayer.

But that does not mean that he did not pray in ways that influenced others powerfully. Because they needed an institutionalized prayer to help them resist their growing opposition, to remind them of what they stood for, and to connect them to the one they began to see as their founder, the Q people somewhat unwittingly preserved some elements of Jesus' own prayers. But contrary to Jesus' intention, Q's preservation of these words resulted in them becoming a part of a recited group prayer. We are now in a position to turn to that material behind the Q Jesus Prayer, prayers that most likely came from Jesus himself.

4

Pieces of Jesus' Prayer

A FRAGMENTED CORE

Finally we have found a trail of material close to the historical Jesus. In the Q Jesus Prayer there is very early Jesus prayer. We are finally in a position to home in on prayer fragments that may well come from Jesus himself.

Although we have seen good reasons to conclude that the formal Jesus prayer found in Q originated with the Q people, this must not stop us from looking more closely at some elements of that prayer. When we unhook specific phrases from its formal unit, we find striking aspects of specific phrases that point toward the historical Jesus.

This chapter will do exactly that. It will take the earliest form of the so-called Lord's Prayer, the Q Jesus prayer, and dismantle it in order to detect any elements which might actually be from the historical Jesus. Some of what emerges from such close examination will be fragments of the prayer life of the historical Jesus. In other cases, the phrases will be found to belong to the Q group itself.

This dismantling will proceed phrase by phrase.

Father

The Q prayer used "Father" rather than the "Our Father in heaven," which latter phrase carries Matthew's typical interest in "heaven." The question becomes, did Jesus pray "Father" or was that phrase coined by Q?

This "Father" phrase most likely came from the Aramaic word for father "Abba." Interestingly enough, the word "Abba" occurs strikingly early and in a wide range of first-century "Christian" texts, all of which were written in Greek. It appears twice in Paul (Rom 8:15 and Gal 4:6) and once in Mark (14:36). Both Mark and Paul took pains in their text to translate "Abba" as "father." Finding the Aramaic word that Jesus would have spoken in preserved Greek texts most likely indicates that followers of Jesus from a wide variety of settings remembered that he spoke to God that way.

One might object that addressing God as "Abba" or "Father" was commonplace, and therefore the presence of the Aramaic "Abba" in the early Greek texts did not necessarily indicate material from Jesus. But that is not the case. "Father" was not a very common way of addressing God in first century Aramaic-speaking Judaism. "Abba" was a standard word for human fathers, but there is little evidence of it being used in reference to God. The early Christian use of "Abba" in Jesus' maternal Aramaic was so infrequently recorded that it most probably reflects Jesus' actual usage.

"Abba," then, is the first prayer fragment that all major scholars agree can be traced with reasonable certainty back to the historical Jesus. I find no reason to doubt this conclusion.

Your Name be Revered

In the Hebrew scriptures and in Jewish prayer the name of God is revered. The eighteen benedictions, said daily as prayer by Jews of the first century, included as the second sentence of the third benediction, "Your name is revered." Many other Jewish prayers of that day speak of the holiness of God's name. Reverence for God's name is also found throughout Hebrew scriptures (e.g. Isa 29:23; Ezek 36:22).

It is almost certain that during his lifetime Jesus said the 18 benedictions as prayer. Even if he did not slavishly speak them every day—as a clever sage might not—he certainly spoke them from time to time. Since these benedictions contain the phrase "Your name is revered," it is clear that Jesus commonly spoke this prayer fragment as well. At least growing up, and most likely in his adult life as well, Jesus surely asked that God's name be revered. He surely uttered this formula in group prayer setting (at a meal, at sundown, in a synagogue), and perhaps prayed it when he was alone.

Let Your Domain Come

The sayings attributed to Jesus contain many references to the basileia/domain/kingdom of God both in the teachings that seem to go back to Jesus and in those added by later gospel writers. How can it be determined whether this simple prayer request that God's basileia come is from Jesus or from later gospel writers?

On the one hand, a prayer by Jesus asking for God's domain or "kingdom" fits the larger picture of Jesus as sage in at least four ways:

1. Jesus' teachings reveal his appetite for and fascination with God's reign over the world. As noted in Chapter 1, God's "basileia" is a major theme in the teachings of the historical Jesus. Of the ninety sayings traced by the Jesus Seminar to the historical Jesus, at least fourteen of them are explicitly about "God's basileia." At least eight others were later associated by the gospel writers with Jesus' idea of God's imperial rule. So it is quite easy to imagine Jesus offering this sentence prayer almost as a sigh of anticipation: "Come on, God, impose this rule of yours" or "Oh God, just let this reign of yours come."

2. We have noted earlier that the way Jesus' teachings refer to God's "basileia" was typical of the ways hellenistic wisdom associated learning with rule. This common idea that a sage "ruled" over the world by being wise situates Jesus' teachings about the "basileia/kingdom" of God within a broader concept of wisdom. Many sages taught about a more intangible reign available only to the one who seeks to understand. As noted earlier, the pervasiveness of sages' proclamations of an intangible and elusive reign makes an astonishingly close fit with many of Jesus' parables and aphorisms. A prayer for this intangible reign belonged to a circle of learners/sages, who understood themselves as kings by virtue of the way their fresh thinking kept them free of conventions that would otherwise rule their lives. Indeed, such a prayer by Jesus must have been at once wry and self-involving. For a sage, asking for God's reign was a way of keeping one's learning quest open-ended and on-going. Such a prayer by a sage would have been spoken in the delightful and risk-taking self-consciousness that only through an openness to learn does one become a part of God's reign.

3. The "basileia" of God in the teachings of Jesus surprises the listener, especially with its implicit and elusive character. Perhaps the saying which captures this dimension best is Thom 113:2–4 (Luke 17:20, 21):

> His disciples said to him, "When will the Father's imperial rule come?"
> "It will not come by watching for it. It will not be said, 'Look, here' or 'Look, there.' Rather, the Father's imperial rule is spread out upon the earth, and people don't see it."

This divine "basileia" did not fit the normal patterns of economic or social convention. According to the core teachings of Jesus, God's domain is like a vineyard owner who pays all his laborers the same wage, even though some worked twelve times as long as others (Matt 20:1–15). Or, even more shocking to a society where having as many sons as possible was a sure sign of God's favor, Jesus saluted the men who "castrated themselves because of Heaven's imperial rule" (Matt 19:12). In a world where wealth also was seen as a sign of God's blessing, Jesus pressed the differentness of God's reign by exclaiming: "How difficult it is for those who have money to enter God's domain!" (Mark 10:23). A prayer for God's rule or domain was then an invocation of surprising learning. Staying open to the combination of surprise and learning is, of course, not easy. Being open to discover all that is hidden around one involves particular kinds of consciousness and risks. Taking internalizing and spiritual steps to allow for and maintain this openness was the rationale for Jesus' prayer that the comprehensive, elusive, and surprising reign of God come.

4. The Scholars Version translation of the key word, "basileia," of this prayer fragment as "imperial rule" (rather than the traditional "kingdom") has broken open one of the key dimensions of both this prayer and Jesus' teachings. Advocating the "kingdom of God" had to have been a satirical commentary and aphoristic twist on the claims and presumptions of the Roman empire. So, the translation "God's imperial rule" (or in this verse, "your imperial rule") helps accent the ironic character of Jesus' proclamation and invocation of God's reign. The coming and presence of God's reign in Jesus' teachings mocked and pre-empted the more obvious imperial rule of Rome. A prayer then for the coming of "your imperial rule" required investing one's self in uncovering this hidden counter movement of God, and challenged others—in a way similar to Jesus' teachings—to invest themselves through prayer in the same counter movement.

There is strong reason then to see Jesus praying "Let your basileia come" as a part of his larger mission as a Galilean sage under Roman rule.

On the other hand, it is just this tight fit with his message that also may indicate that it was a prayer summary of his message created Jesus' followers. In this way, the prayer phrase "Let your basileia come" could well have been composed by the Q community, to serve as both a summary and reminder of what they were living for. Because of the shortness of this prayer phrase, there are few fingerprints left on it. It is impossible to find within this short prayer phrase strong evidence whether it was Jesus' own prayer or a good summary by his followers. Thus afforded the option, I will classify it with the possible prayer fragments attributable to the historical Jesus. The case for it being a prayer fragment from Jesus himself is less strong than that for "Abba" and "May your name be revered," but there is no great reason to discount it as having been prayed by Jesus.

Give Us the Bread We Need for Today

With this prayer fragment a relatively major difference between Matthew and Luke comes into view. Whereas Matthew has "Give us the bread we need for today," Luke has a more general "Give us the bread we need day by day."

Most scholars agree that this difference points to Luke's re-working of the prayer phrase to make it more suitable for a larger gentile audience. But by making it simply a prayer for bread for one's life, Luke has taken the punch-line out of the prayer. In Matthew's (most likely earlier) version, the surprising twist typical of Jesus' teachings remained intact.

As illustrated in the sketch at the beginning of this book, the prayer "Give us the bread we need for today" caught one by surprise. Although at first blush appealing to impoverished Galilean peasants who longed for justice and adequate food, it quickly challenged these peasants to live in the moment without worrying what tomorrow brought.

As also noted in the opening sketch, to pray "Give us the bread we need (just) for today" also echoed the life style of the early sages, who wandered from village to village, depending on people's generosity (and God's mercy) to feed and shelter them. Luke's more general "Give us the bread we need day by day" was much less about such sages risking lack of food and more about ordinary householders who prayed conventionally for bread at their tables.

These considerations point to Matthew's "Give us the bread we need (just) for today" as going back to both Q and Jesus himself. Here is yet another prayer fragment which sounds like the aphoristic sage whose teachings tweaked hearers with surprise and embarrassment. And, once again, a fragment from the Q Jesus Prayer makes much more sense as a prayer of the historical Jesus when it is taken out of the larger prayer and experienced as a prayer of Jesus on its own.

Forgive Our Debts to the Extent We Have Forgiven Those in Debt to Us

In this prayer fragment as well, an important difference between Luke and Matthew can be observed, and a similar conclusion drawn that Matthew has preserved Q and the historical Jesus much more clearly.

The difference is striking, and at first puzzling to the reader in our time. Whereas Luke had Jesus praying "Forgive our sins, since we too forgive everyone in debt to us," Matthew had "Forgive our debts to the extent that we have forgiven those in debt to us." In other words, Matthew had Jesus praying about debts, while Luke made the prayer about the forgiveness of sins. From the perspective of Americans today, praying about the forgiveness of debts seems much more obscure than praying for forgiveness of sins. At first blush, then, one would want to think that Jesus prayed about the "more important" issue of sins being forgiven. This turns out not to be the case.

Indebtedness was one of the major social and economic problems of first century Israel. The peasant farmers and the merchants in the towns and villages were constantly in danger of falling into serious debt to the landed class and to the urban elite. Farmers, who by and large planted small sections of land, were subject to the whims of weather and the market. Merchants often fell behind in their accounts for very similar reasons.

Although these cycles of indebtedness were acute in the first century, the peasant class of israel had rarely been out of danger of debt during the previous twelve hundred years. Even before the monarchy in Israel, tribal peasants were threatened with foreclosure by the Canaanite cities. The Hebrew prophets regularly came to the defense of poor farmers, whose crops were often not sufficient to keep them out of debt. This long history of indebtedness among the peasants probably had its roots in the less than ideal growing conditions in Israel, coupled with economic pressures from urban centers of commerce.

So, to have prayed about indebtedness made a great deal of sense in first century Galilee. Our initial reaction to the obscureness of a prayer for release from indebtedness was probably Luke's as well. Luke, more at home in much more gentile and urban surroundings, most likely changed the original prayer about indebtedness to one about forgiveness of sins, a more general human dilemma than debts.

Understanding all this makes Matthew's "Forgive us our debts to the extent to which we have forgiven those indebted to us" much more evocative of both Q and the historical Jesus, whose common milieu was the peasant class in Galilee.

Similarly a prayer like "Forgive us our debts to the extent to which we have forgiven those indebted to us" was much more in the style of Jesus, the aphoristic sage. It did not simply ask for forgiveness of debts, but added the twist of mutual forgiveness of debts. It prompted each person listening to the prayer to think about his or her own role and responsibility.

Here again a prayer fragment detached from the larger Q prayer, appears very much in character with the historical Jesus.

And Please Don't Subject Us to Test After Test

The wisdom tradition in Israel gives ample examples of sages praying not to be subjected to ordeals (see Box 5). Since there was ample precedent for either Jesus or the Q people to pray for release from too strong a challenge, this prayer fragment can be assigned to the very early stages of Jesus material, before Matthew or Luke wrote. Our task is to decide whether this prayer sentence comes from Q's embattled sages or Jesus.

Chapter three outlined the ways in which the Q people became embattled in their Galilean villages because of their aggressive pursuit of hidden wisdom and their attacks on conventional family, economic, and religious life. Their devotion to the discovery of God's domain spread out on the earth, a quest they had shared with Jesus before he died, had begun to backfire on them. Their long-term and unswerving commitment to this

---

Box 5: Wisdom Prayers Prior to Jesus Asking for
Help in the Midst of Ordeals

Lord father and master of my life,
Do not abandon me to their whims,
Do not let me fall because of them.
    —Ben Sirach (Ecclesiasticus 23:1)

God, examine me and know my heart.
Test me and know my concerns.
Make sure that I am not on my way to ruin.
    —Ps 139:23

God of our ancestors, Lord of mercy ...
grant me Wisdom, consort of your throne
and do not reject me from the number of your children.
Send her forth from your throne of glory to help me
and to toil with me.
    —Wisdom of Solomon 9:1a, 4, 10a

My lord father,
Do not desert me in the days of ordeal.
    —Ben Sirach (Ecclesiasticus 51:10)

way of life caused families, synagogues, and the wealthy to become irritated at the way they pressed their criticism and flaunted their independence.

The Q document actually has evidence of such conflicts erupting. In Q 12:11 there are instructions for such a controversy: "When they make you appear in synagogues and haul you before rulers and authorities, don't worry about how or in what ways you should defend yourself or what you should say. The holy spirit will teach you at that very moment what you ought to say" (Luke 12:11).

Such instructions were most likely intended for Q people who were called before synagogue and other authorities for their criticism and behavior. Passages from the Q document indicate that although the Q people did not appear as a threat to Roman authorities, they were regularly getting in trouble with authorities from the village institutions they frequented.

This is the context that makes most sense for the prayer fragment "And please don't subject us to test after test." The Q people were in fact being subjected to test after test, and the level of conflict was becoming greater they had bargained for. They needed relief. It makes sense that they would put into the prayer to help them stabilize them in a trying time the plea not to be put to the test time after time.

So this final prayer fragment from the Q Jesus Prayer makes less sense in the mouth of the historical Jesus than in the trials of the Q people during their thirty year pursuit of Jesus' wisdom.

The result of our close examination of the individual phrases of the Q Jesus prayer is that when they are uncoupled from the prayer unit, a surprising number of them seem to show strong affinities with the historical Jesus. Although the Lord's Prayer—or even its parent prayer, the Q Jesus prayer—cannot be from Jesus himself, it clearly contains important fragments of Jesus' prayer life. Indeed all but one of the phrases in the Q Jesus Prayer can be traced back to the historical Jesus.

Are these fragments significant? Can five fragments before and behind the Lord's Prayer tell us much about how Jesus prayed? These questions can be answered only by trying to locate these prayer fragments in specific settings of Jesus' life. It is this task which the next five chapters address.

5

Abba • Father

By calling God "Father" Jesus made people think twice. It may surprise us, but calling God "Father" in Jesus' day was not a standard way of talking about or praying to God. Although it was not completely unheard of, it was fairly rare. Saying "Father" to God would likely have produced something between a slight wrinkle on the brow and a bright twinkle in the eye of any who heard it.

Such a response would be due partly to Jesus' use of the Aramaic "Abba." Where Jesus lived, most prayers were said in Hebrew. Aramaic was Jesus' mother tongue and the language spoken in the villages. Hebrew was used only as a sacred language, similar to the way Latin was used in the Roman Catholic church before Vatican II. So Jesus' use of the colloquial Aramaic "Abba" for God was at least mildly provocative.

Although the Greek text of both gospel versions of "The Lord's Prayer" does not use "Abba," this Aramaic word does appear in several places in the Greek New Testament (in the writings of Mark and Paul), suggesting that later Christians retained Jesus' Aramaic word in their own prayers. This, as noted in the last chapter, is a major reason to think that Jesus himself used the Aramaic "Abba."

Jesus not only referred to God as "Abba/Father," but also prayed to God as "Abba/Father." However, when we consider the gospels' context for Jesus' addressing on God as "Abba," we run into a problem. Luke and Matthew (who were borrowing from Q) used Jesus' "Abba" as the opening invocation of a formalized prayer known to Christians as The Lord's Prayer and, as we have seen, first formulated by the Q community. As noted in the preceding chapter, it is very unlikely that Jesus said any version of this particular prayer. Rather, The Lord's Prayer was most likely composed a generation after Jesus.

Furthermore, it is highly doubtful that Jesus ever taught anyone how to pray, much less to memorize and repeat The Lord's Prayer! When the core sayings of the historical Jesus are examined as a whole—as they can be in this book—the Jesus who emerges does not seem interested in teaching others to pray. Likely he would have even opposed the idea of teaching others particular words to recite as a prayer. Of the ninety sayings that the Jesus Seminar attributed to the historical Jesus, no others—beside five of the eight phrases in what eventually came to be the Lord's Prayer—even mention prayer. There is no teaching of Jesus in these ninety sayings that recommends prayer or even alludes to it. Even more to the point, the teacher Jesus that emerges from these other eighty-five sayings is an aphorist—one who deliberately and specifically challenges a rote and unreflective approach to life. The Jesus of these ninety sayings was not interested in founding or even supporting institutions, whether they were religious, family, economic or political institutions.

So Jesus' prayer of "Abba/Father" is most likely just a fragment from prayers that he prayed. While we cannot reconstruct what the rest of his "Abba" prayers said, the fact that this Aramaic word resurfaces in so many New Testament passages about prayer is powerful evidence for locating this key word in Jesus' personal prayer life.

What Jesus Meant by Abba

What then could "Abba/Father" have meant in the prayers of the historical Jesus? In the context of the other ninety authentic sayings of Jesus, "Abba" points toward a spirituality that calls traditional dependencies into question and casts oneself on the care of God. Conventional wisdom takes it for granted that people should rely on wealth, family, temple, and nation. However, Jesus' core sayings regularly criticized dependence on these conventions, and invoked trust in the more basic fabric of life that God provides.

> "Don't fret about your life—what you're going to eat or drink—or about your body—what you're going to wear. There is more to living than food and clothing, isn't there? Take a look at the birds of the air ...."
>
> —Matt 6:25–30

Such teachings heralding this more basic trust were companion pieces to those that challenged dependency on wealth (such as Luke 6:20 and Mark 10:25), family (such as Luke 14:26 and Matt 12:48–50), scholarly prestige (such as Mark 12:38–39), or religion (such as Mark 2:27–28 and Luke 18:10–14).

God then was the source of strength and nurture in Jesus' core teachings, but this was not a God who was enmeshed in and allied to systems of wealth, family, and religion. This was an "Abba/Father," a God invoked over against the conventions of economy, nation, temple, and clan.

Since Jesus did not mandate that the title of "Abba/Father" be used all the time, it most likely emerged as a clever dimension to his challenge of family privileges and convention. Look, for instance, at the way the traditions of family are deftly redefined by the "Abba/Father"hood of God in this core saying of Jesus:

"My mother and my brothers—whoever are they?... Here are my mother and my brothers. For whoever does the will of my Father in heaven, that's my brother and sister and mother" (Matt 12:48–50).

In first century Galilee family was the primary form of "social security." That is, it was bonds of kinship that provided a safety net for the needy and the aged or suffered health or business disasters. But for Jesus, reliance on traditional family ties was an impediment to a lifestyle that trusts in the God beyond family conventions. Seeing God as "Abba/Father" was a clever combination of challenge to family tradition and evocation of a new trust in the divine fabric of life itself. Calling out to God as "Abba/Father" replaced one's reliance on the family systems of privilege, inheritance, and honor. Such a prayer let go of these conventions and expressed Jesus' dependence on God alone. Those listening to his "Abba" prayers were no doubt aware that he was replacing tangible family security with a much more intangible "reign of God."

Did Jesus Grow Up Without a Father?

The use of "Abba/Father" by the historical Jesus may well have had some very personal roots. Many biblical scholars now think that Jesus was probably raised without a father. The complete lack of reference to Joseph in the Gospel of Mark (even though Mary has a significant role in this gospel) and the very brief treatment of Joseph in the birth stories in Matthew and Luke point away from an historical Joseph. Similarly, a number of scholars have seen the motif of the virgin birth in Matthew and Luke as a defense against charges of illegitimacy resulting from common knowledge that Jesus had only a mother.

If this were the case, Jesus—both as a child and and adult—would likely have suffered the taunts of being an "illegitimate" child, and come to an understanding of himself that transcended the social slur of "bastard." For a person, whose lack of father had been thrown in his face for so long, praying to God as "Abba/Father" might signal a new self-understanding beyond the oppressive conventions of society. It may also have been a way of cleverly tossing the "bastard" insult back in the faces of those with traditional family values.

In such a situation Jesus praying "Abba" helped him confirm himself as someone worthy, despite the shame of not having a human father in a patriarchal society. Perhaps it was not having a father that taught him about the pretense and limitedness of family-based security. Having to let go of such family securities may have pointed him toward the hidden and intangible care of God—a path not so obvious to those enmeshed in the strong claims of village family loyalties. Naming God "Abba/Father" in public prayer confirmed his new worth before God in the same breath as it challenged others' dependencies on the conventional system of family security.

Jesus Uses Abba in Prayer

How, when, and where did Jesus pray "Abba?" To illustrate the line of thinking developed in this chapter, the sketches, similar to the one at the beginning of the book, place Abba/Father in imagined prayer settings of the first century Galilean Jesus.

SKETCH ONE

He was a childhood playmate of Jesus. When Jesus ran into him on the road at the edge of the field, they both smiled, remembering how they had played together at the nearby lake years ago.

After the usual greetings and small talk, the friend broached an uncomfortable subject:

"You know, Jesus, how my father has always preferred my younger brother to me. I'm beginning to worry about my inheritance. As eldest son, I have the right to twice as much of this land as my brother. But as we get older, my father continues to assign both of us equal portions to work on. I'm afraid that is an indication that my father plans on dividing this land equally between us."

"Have you talked to your father about this?" Jesus asked.

"No, but I am planning to. I think it's time that I lay claim to my formal rights as the eldest son of my father. But I'm not sure about the timing. What do you think?"

Jesus was still for a moment.

The friend continued, "If I go to my father now and lay claim to the land too quickly, I'm afraid my father will be upset. On the other hand, I keep worrying that he will not give me my due. And I'm counting on the larger part of the land to support my own children and wife. So I'm leaning toward going to him, and saying 'Abba, I am your eldest son.' He will certainly understand that as a gentle claim to my inheritance."

Jesus said, "Let's take a walk down to the lake, where we used to play."

As they began strolling toward the lake, the friend continued to fret about his future, his relationship to his father and brother, and the lack of rain in the past month. When they reached the lake, there was still a strip of land Jesus' friend stood to inherit within view.

Jesus said to his friend, "Look out at the lake with me."

"I remember when we kids tried to float out away from shore on logs we had tied together. You fell in once."

"That was so much fun," Jesus replied. "Look at how the sun is shimmering on the inlet over there."

Then Jesus reached out and touched his friend and said, "So here's what I think about your father and claiming the land for yourself."

"Oh good, I thought you might have an idea."

"Look out at this lake we both love, and say with me. Abba."

"What?" Asked the puzzled friend.

"Here goes," Jesus said and then shouted out to the lake, "Abba."

"Try it again." Jesus said in reponse to the friend not having done it. Then Jesus shouted "Abba" again, and the friend mumbled it with him at least out of deference to his friend.

"This is great," Jesus said, and then shouted again out over the lake, "Abba, I am your eldest son."

"Try that one," Jesus said, and then they both shouted to the lakeside, "Abba, I am your eldest son."

Smiling sheepishly, the friend queried, "So are you sure that I'm going to inherit twice as many of the fish in the lake as my brother?"

Jesus smiled also and said, "You may have to share them with a few of the gulls, but I think there will be more than enough for you."

"Just to humor me," said the friend, "How about shouting with me in the direction of my father's field?" They turned around and shouted with full voice.

They began strolling back to the road, reminiscing about their childhood and musing about the weather. Back at the road, they smiled again.

"Thanks for the prayer." the friend said.

"Don't fight too much with the birds over your inheritance." Jesus replied as they parted.

SKETCH TWO

The village had been divided for some time over the question of what to do about broken water cistern. So it was natural that the subject came up at the banquet celebrating of the wine merchant's birthday. They had finished the meal, the first round of drinks had been served, and nearly everyone was talking about how to pay for the repair of this vital part of the village's water supply.

The wine merchant himself and several of the wealthier farmers, were in favor of all residents paying something into a common fund so that the cistern could be replaced. A number of others, generally less wealthy, could not see spending that much money.

Just then the servant announced that several of the itinerant sages from Nazareth had arrived to join the party. It was not the first time these rather eccentric sages from the neighboring village had wandered into a local celebration.

"I really don't want them at my party," the wine merchant shouted, "They make me uncomfortable with all their weird sayings. And we're right in the middle of an important village discussion."

By this time the sages were standing in the doorway of the banquet room.

"Go away. We are in the middle of village business here." shouted the farmer friend of the wine merchant.

"But turning them away is not correct observance of our village's tradition of hospitality." said another farmer.

"Oh, yes, it is," said the wine merchant, "I happen to know that one of these sages is a bastard, born out of wedlock. According to our traditions, such a person cannot demand our hospitality, but must beg for it."

"Is this true?" the hospitality-conscious farmer asked of the sages.

"I am Jesus, son of Mary." one of the sages replied.

"If you have no father, then get out of here." the wine merchant's friend yelled.

But the one farmer persisted in his attempts to keep the peace: "OK. Perhaps he should not interrupt our important discussion. But since he is a sage, let us hear a brief teaching from him as he stands at the door." The others, eager to get back to the cistern matter, agreed.

"A prayer for you and your fathers," said the sage. And then stretched out his hands in the traditional prayer stance, raised his eyes toward the ceiling and spoke in a normal tone: "Abba, bless our family. Abba, bless this family. Abba, bless our family. Abba. Abba. Amen."

The other sages had grins on their faces as they left. The company was quiet for several minutes after they had gone, then slowly the conversation returned to the matter at hand.

Conclusions

Placing the prayer fragment "Abba/Father"—now detached from any form of the Lord's Prayer—in the context of Jesus' life as a Galilean sage not only shows how much it belonged to Jesus, but also tells a great deal about the character of Jesus' prayer life. We begin to understand not just a particular word Jesus used in prayer, but a whole strategy of prayer that challenged the one praying and those listening to re-think and re-situate themselves. This kind of prayer fit into Jesus' larger calling as sage. It integrated his spirituality with his quest for wisdom, his social status, and his particular personal background.

Two conclusions that others have drawn about Jesus praying "Abba" may not be as appropriate. First of all, we need to challenge the conclusion of much of traditional Christianity that Jesus' use of Abba validates an exclusively male picture. Although one cannot debate that the great majority of references to God in Jesus' Galilee were male-gendered, it is much less clear that Jesus' use of the term Abba/Father was meant to endorse the maleness of God or exclusive male reference to God.

As this book's treatment of the Abba prayer has shown, "Abba" seems to have been much more unconventional than an endorsement of God as male would have been. The use of "Abba" in prayer made Jesus' prayer more colloquial and less traditional than most other prayer of his time, and may well have been a specific processing by Jesus of his own status as social outcast. With these factors in mind, it is difficult to see "Abba" as upholding the traditional male grip on power. Similarly, in the gospel teachings of Jesus (although not in the ones we can attribute to the historical Jesus) Jesus was also portrayed as talking about God in female terms. In Luke 7:35, for instance, Jesus was portrayed as claiming the wisdom movement's female picture of the divine, when he says: "Wisdom is justified by her children."

Another fairly popular interpretation of Jesus' use of "Abba" in prayer needs to be challenged. Influenced mostly by the mid-twentieth century writings of German scholar Joachim Jeremias, many commentators interpret "Abba" as an intimate expression of little children for their "Daddy." Such a line of interpretation has promoted the notion that Jesus' image of God was that of an approachable, loving "Daddy," not a distant, angry authority. Occasionally such a "loving Daddy" is unfairly contrasted with allegedly less kindly images of God in the Hebrew scriptures.

This reading of a "loving Daddy" into Jesus' usage of "Abba" cannot be justified by textual evidence within the New Testament. The three occurrences of the word (Mark14:36, Rom 8:15, Gal 4:6) all picture adults in very adult situations crying out to God. In both Rom 8:15 and Gal 4:6, gentile followers of Jesus Christ cry out to "Abba" to claim their "sonship" before God. This is much more reminiscent of adult sons claiming their inheritance than little children being embraced by a loving Daddy. In both these texts the issue is whether gentiles also can become "sons" of the Jewish God in the new Jesus Christ movement. Thus the use of "Abba" was almost a legal term used by gentile Christians to claim of their spiritual "sonship" in Jesus Christ. Similarly Mark 14:36 pictures Jesus in the garden of Gethsemane crying out to his "Abba" in his darkest hour of decision.This hardly suggests the interaction of a small child and a loving Daddy. If anything, it was a picture of Jesus coming into his adulthood, agreeing to a major role his "Abba" had for him as an adult.

Jesus' "Abba" prayers then had to do with neither his endorsement of a male image of God nor his picture of God as a loving Daddy. Rather, as laid out and illustrated earlier in this chapter, this Abba prayer is our first example of the clever, image-breaking, and intensely social sage at work.

6

Your Name Be Revered

It would have been nearly impossible for Jesus not to have prayed that God's name be revered and honored as holy. This sentence belongs to a number of traditional prayers that almost every Jew in Galilee said regularly.

As we have seen, "Your name is holy," was the third of the Eighteen Benedictions said in first-century Galilee. "Magnified and sanctified be his great name" and "Your name, O Lord our God, shall be hallowed" are found in two other traditional Jewish prayers from the same period. In each case the root words in Hebrew and Greek can be translated "holy," "hallowed," "revered," or "sanctified."

Whether it was at dusk in a courtyard where Jesus and his partner sages had been invited to bed down for the night, or at a meal where a traditional blessing was offered, we can quite easily picture Jesus praying "Your name be revered." Most likely in such settings he would have said one of these traditional hallowings of God's name with others. The level of consciousness at which Jesus and the others recited these traditional prayers probably varied according to the occasion. Similarly contemporary Americans vary in how much attention they pay to the meaning of "The Star Spangled Banner" when it is sung at a sporting event. Often the traditional prayers were said because they—like the national anthem—belonged to the way the culture made its way through particular moments.

There are no other references to the holiness of God's name in the core teachings of Jesus, so we have no indication that this was a key idea in Jesus' teachings. It is more likely that this was a part of Jesus' consciousness simply because he belonged to Galilean Jewish culture and prayed together with other Jews.

A Joke?

This phrase, "Your name be revered," eventually was put together with Jesus' "Abba/Father" prayer in a clever and provocative manner. It is unclear whether Jesus himself prayed "Abba/Father, your name be revered" or whether the generation after Jesus put these two prayers of his together. Whoever did that was in a humorous mood, and produced one of the better jokes of early Christianity. It is, unfortunately, a joke that modern readers do not get.

The joke goes something like this. When first-century Jews generally gave reverence to God's name, they were referring to a particular, special, and sacred word that was God's name. That name was then and still is thought to be so special and alive with the divine that it was and is rarely said by Jews. That name today is usually pronounced (by those who dare) "Yahweh," and was pronounced "Jehovah" until recently. The transliterated Hebrew consonants are YHWH, and the pronunciation depends on which vowels are inserted and where they are placed. But in any case, when first-century Jews referred to the revering of God's name, they were thinking of (but not pronouncing) a particular name, "Yahweh."

When Jesus or his followers first prayed "Abba/Father, your name be revered," they were giving God another name. This other name was a common Aramaic word, one thrown around every day in every household. That is, it was not in the sacred language of Hebrew, and it was not treated as any kind of special name. Associating "Abba" with the very special holy name of God (everyone knew that "Yahweh," not "Abba" was the holy name of God) was almost a contradiction in terms. Here is the point where a first-century person would get the joke and laugh, or get the point and feel offended.

This ironic association of the common word for father with the revered name of God was certainly jarring in the way many of the early Christian wisdom sayings were. Just as Jesus' association of blessedness or happiness with the poor and hungry was shocking, so was the prayer "Abba/Father, your name be revered." The unexpected combination surprised people into rethinking what was and was not holy. As a prayer, it called upon people to put God and reverence in a much broader perspective. Such a prayer fit well with Jesus' teachings which, in a religious climate where such comparisons were rare, consistently cited the poor and children as images of God's reign. This two-sentence prayer—like Jesus' parables and aphorisms—expanded people's vision of what was important and holy.

A Galilean Scene

How to understand the potential impact of this aphoristic prayer, "Abba, your name be revered." Imagine the following scenario:

A SKETCH

The three Galilean sages had walked farther from their home villages than usual than day. They had struck up a conversation with two farmers headed for Jerusalem, and walked a good thirty miles while talking. Now it was dusk. The farmers had gone on to the next village where they had relatives. The three sages looked around for someplace to stay. This was a fairly common dilemma for them, but they had never been to this particular village.

They had hailed two people in the marketplace to see if they could stay overnight with them, and had been turned down. But another merchant had overheard them and directed them to the house at the top of the hill, which—according to the merchant—had hosted a couple of wandering sages just three weeks ago.

So they walked into the courtyard of that house at the brow of the hill. The chickens scattered as they approached. Several unkempt children looked up from their evening chores. A woman in her fifties approached them.

"Peace to you," she said, "Are you looking for someone?"

"Peace also to you," the elder sage replied, "We are actually looking for a place to stay the night. We are teachers, and would gladly share some wisdom in exchange for a place to sleep and the bread we need for today."

"Well, we have no space in the house. But you are welcome to sleep here in the courtyard," she replied. "I'm not sure we have time for any wisdom tonight, but we'd love to have you join us in our evening prayers, which we hope to begin any time now."

"We are happy to share the space with the chickens," another sage added. The woman gestured to one corner of the courtyard where they could bed down.

"Oh, look here come my two sons. We can say the evening prayers here in the courtyard. Josiah, go call your wife and the children, and we can pray now."

While the sages briefly inspected the courtyard corner designated their sleeping quarters, some eleven people emerged from the house and stalls. As they gathered, most of them greeted the sages.

Josiah, who may have been the woman's son, began with the traditional two benedictions, and then turned to the sages, and asked, "Would one of you continue with the third benediction?"

The shorter of the sages took a step forward, while continuing to rock back and forth in the traditional prayer rhythms, and spoke: "Magnificent and holy is your name." The second sage quickly added, "Abba." The first sage smiled and began to repeat his blessing, "Magnificent and holy is your name." The second sage said louder, "Hear us, Abba." The third sage added, "So holy is your name." The second sage said again, "Abba."

By this time the children were laughing. Josiah was scratching his head. The woman who had let the sages in was smiling. Josiah spoke: "Why in the middle of praising God's holy name is one of you talking about your father? Don't you know that the holiness of God's name is very special?"

The older woman asked: "Are you suggesting that God's name is Abba? Surely you know that Abba is not a holy name for anybody. It's just the way we talk every day."

Josiah added," If we can call God Abba, then we can also call God "Uncle" or "Aunt" or "Friend."

One of the children, now having brought her laughter under control, jumped in with "Can I call God my sister?"

Her bigger brother responded, "No, I heard that we are not supposed to say God's name at all. Isn't that true, Mommy?"

The shorter sage stopped rocking in prayer, since by now most everyone else was responding to his "Abba, may your name be revered" prayer. He said, "Well, it's just something I've been thinking about. I'm glad for your questions and responses. Why don't we just go ahead with the rest of the benedictions. Maybe we can talk about it when we have some bread together."

He and the others started their rhythmic rocking again. Josiah picked up with the fourth benediction. The shorter sage said the fifth and sixth benedictions. And before anyone realized it, the prayer time was over.

Conclusions

Detaching these two prayer fragments from the larger "Lord's Prayer" has shown clearly that both the traditional Jewish prayer "Your name be revered" and the clever "Abba, your name be revered" fit well with our portrait of Jesus, the Galilean sage. It is then quite certain Jesus prayed "Your name be revered," and relatively certain that he prayed "Abba, your name be revered." The project of piecing together a picture of Jesus at prayer from the fragments behind The Lord's Prayer is gaining momentum.

7

Let Your Domain Come

As a prayer on its own—detached from the Q Jesus prayer and the Lord's Prayer, and re-situated as an independent prayer of the historical Jesus—"let your basileia come" turns out to be a prayer with multiple meanings and applications. (For a review of Jesus' teachings about the basileia/kingdom of God see chap. 1, pp. 21–24) As a sentence prayer, it could have had a number of very evocative meanings for Jesus and those with whom he prayed.

Praying In Search of Wisdom

This brief plea that God's rule come could have acted as a standard companion to Jesus' quirky "kingdom" parables about God's basileia/ reign, which themselves were intended to evoke and illustrate the way the God's domain was already here or at least just around the corner. Praying "let your basileia come" could have been the exclamation point on sayings which compared God's reign to a mustard seed, the poor, or children. If one could see the "kingdom" in a woman using yeast or an employer paying the workers in a surprising way, a request for the vision to see this "basileia" clearly would be in order.

As we saw in the presentation that "let your basileia come" was a prayer fragment of the historical Jesus, a prayer for this intangible reign fit perfectly into a circle of learners and sages. Indeed, such prayer by Jesus must have been at once wry and self-involving. Asking for God's reign as a sage was a way of keeping one's learning quest open-ended and on-going. Such a prayer by a sage would have been spoken in the delightful and risk-taking self-consciousness that it is through one's own open-ness to learn that one becomes a part of God's reign.

Wisdom, Basileia, and Prayer Come Together

To see how Jesus' prayer fragment invoking the "kingdom" suits the context of a sage's search for wisdom, consider the following scenario:

A STORY

Propped against the well in the market square was a paralyzed woman of about forty. She did little other than observe the market activity, but occasionally she would beg from a likely donor. The sages from the next village, after bantering with a visiting scribe, meandered over to the woman who was now lying down.

One of the sages spoke to her, "Tell me what you know."

"That's a hell of way to begin a conversation. I know that I'm not sure I like you guys," she responded.

"Well, peace to you in any case," another sage said. "But we would really like to hear some wisdom from you."

Another sage added, "That's what we do. We look for wisdom. And, we think you have some."

"All day long, I am mocked. Just leave me alone, and don't make me the butt of your clever debates," the woman said.

The first sage came back, "We really are not mocking you. But let me tell you a story to show you our good will."

"Just so it's not too long," the woman shot back.

The first sage took the opening: "Once somebody planted some seeds, and then forgot about them. That person worked on other things, slept and carried on his business. All the while the seeds were growing, and producing a great harvest."

"That reminds me of some things that have happened to me. But I'm not sure what you're driving at," the woman said. At this point several other people from the vegetable stall stopped by to join the conversation.

The fourth sage jumped in, "We're not always sure either what we're getting at. But we'd like to hear what you've been thinking about." Someone from the meat stall came for some water at the well, and stopped to listen in.

"I've been wondering about my daughter," the woman said. "She seems to be so dreamy these days. I wonder what makes a person that way. Sometimes it makes me mad that she is not helping me more. Sometimes I am attracted to the far-away look that drifts across her face."

The third sage mused, "Well, it's hard to know when to be practical and when to think wild thoughts, isn't it. Does your daughter take after you with her dreaminess?"

"Who knows where it comes from? She has so many ways that are so different than mine. On the other hand, part of me really identifies with her. The funny thing is that I'm probably most attracted to those parts of her that are less like me."

The second sage pressed a bit, "We tend to believe that there is nothing hidden that won't be revealed, nothing puzzling that can't be learned about. Do you feel like you're learning anything from your daughter?" At this point a couple of the bystanders walked away, muttering about not having time to spend listening to a bunch of losers talking about nothing.

"You never know who can teach you stuff, do you? said the paralytic woman. "Sometimes I think just looking around the marketplace teaches me as much as anything else. Although I'm not sure if it helps me get out of this mess I'm in ..."

"Well, maybe some of those thoughts while staring at the people and animals around here do give you some kind of overview of what life is about," the third stage speculated.

"Let your kingdom come," another sage said.

"What?" asked the woman, "What did you say?"

"Let your kingdom come," he replied.

"My kingdom? I don't have a kingdom," the woman shot back.

"It's a kind of prayer we sometimes say while we're in the middle of learning stuff," said the first sage.

"Oh, so it's not my kingdom. It's God's kingdom," said the woman.

"I don't know," said the one sage, "Maybe it's yours and God's together. What were you going to say about learning from the marketplace?"

"Oh, I forget. But here's a story that's been coming up in my head."

"Let your kingdom come," the same sage said.

"Oh, shut up. And let her tell the story," the third sage responded.

She launched in: "There was this guy who got robbed on the road, let's say, the road from Jerusalem to Jericho. He was lying in the ditch. I know about lying in ditches, let me tell you. And along came a priest, and the priest walked by. On the other side of the road, no less. Then a scholar came by. He just looked the other way. Then a Samaritan—I hope you all aren't prejudiced—a Samaritan came along. He stopped, put the guy on his donkey, and took him all the way to town. He paid for somebody to take care of the guy that got robbed, and then just left."

The first sage said, "Amazing stuff."

The third sage said to the second, "Watch it! I don't want to hear that kingdom prayer again."

One of the bystanders asked the fourth sage, "What are you guys trying to do? Do you do healings?"

"Not really. I know that you may have heard stories. But I've never seen any of us heal. We just have discovered that many people like this woman really know a great deal. We like to talk with them, so that we can learn and they can realize how much they belong."

"So is there something spiritual in what you are doing?" The bystander asked.

"Learning for us is always spiritual. Learning makes us a part of a bigger picture. Some of us like to say, 'The kingdom of God is spread out upon the earth, and no one sees it.'"

The first sage was launching into another story. The woman had pushed herself up to a sitting position. The third sage was interested in hearing more about the woman's daughter. The second sage still seemed poised to interject his kingdom prayer. A couple of other people headed toward the well to get some water. The fourth sage continued explaining his thoughts to the bystander who had asked about healing.

Praying for the New Social Basileia

Partly because of its elusive yet intriguing character, Jesus' "basileia" teaching seems ideally suited for use in prayer. Jesus could have well prayed "let your basileia come" in so many social circumstances where he knew that the quirky kingdom he was proclaiming would turn people's lives upside down. Seeing how often Jesus seems to have talked about God's reign or domain, it is quite easy to imagine Jesus saying this sentence prayer almost as a sigh of anticipation: "Come on, God, impose this rule of yours" or "Oh God, just let this reign of yours come."

This divine "basileia" did not fit easily into the normal patterns of economy or social convention. God's domain is like—according to the core teachings of Jesus—a vineyard owner who pays all his laborers the same wage, even though some worked twelve times as long as others (Matt 20:1–15). Or, even more shocking to a society where having as many sons as possible was a sure sign of God's favor, Jesus saluted men who "castrated themselves because of Heaven's imperial rule" (Matt 19:12). In a world where wealth was seen as a sign of God's blessing, Jesus pressed the differentness of God's reign by exclaiming: "How difficult it is for those who have money to enter God's domain!" (Mark 10:23). A prayer for God's rule or domain was then an invocation of surprising learning. Staying open to the combination of surprise and learning is, of course, not easy. Being open to discover all that is hidden in the world around one involves particular kinds of consciousness and risks. Taking internalizing and spiritual steps to allow for and maintain this openness was the rationale for Jesus' prayer that the comprehensive, elusive, and surprising reign of God come. Many would be taken aback by someone praying, "let your basileia come" in the middle of social situations in which workers, families, and guardians of the economy were expecting a conventional order. Such an invocation challenged the hearers and those praying to re-situate their own allegiances toward God by changing the ways they acted toward one another.

Finally, a prayer for the coming of "your imperial rule" in the situation of a people colonialized by Rome was just a little short of a call to revolution. That it was said by a sage, who had no sword and probably looked a bit bedraggled, did not make Rome nervous. And the fact that it was a prayer rather than a manifesto perhaps also lessened the threat to Roman rule. But the point was obvious. This sage was asking God to come and overthrow Rome. Surely this prayer was sometimes heard this way. Saying this kind of prayer in the public market or even at a banquet would have certainly evoked hopes for political freedom and justice for many who heard or prayed along. Of course, as it became clear to these same people what kind of "basileia" Jesus was asking for (one that was present, but elusively so), this prayer made revolution both a political act and one that called for change within one's self.

Confrontation and the Basileia Prayer

Once again the way such fragments such "let your basileia come" can help us understand the character of Jesus' prayer life can be illustrated in the following imagined scene:

A STORY

It was early morning as the unit of Roman soldiers moved into Nazareth. Two mounted centurions and a company of fourteen others on foot. The village was just stirring to consciousness. But the sights and sounds of the soldiers soon had many villagers unusually awake.

It was not clear what the soldiers wanted. They could be simply stopping for water. They could be doing the semi-annual harrassment of the countryside, just to keep people afraid. That sometimes resulted in an arbitrary crucifixion or two, but sometimes no more than some beatings. Or they could be up to something more secretive.

When Jesus stepped out of his family's house, he saw a couple of his sage friends across the way, and walked over to them. A couple of the soldiers watched him stroll up the street.

Much sooner than anyone could have expected, Jesus shouted: "Let your empire come." Then his friends joined him and shouted so loud that it brought a good dozen people to their windows: "Let your empire come."

Three neighbors came scurrying over to the group of sages.

"What are you doing?" said the first neighbor breathlessly. "Are you trying to irritate them by shouting at them? And what in the world does that mean, 'Let your empire come?'"

They started to shout their phrase again, but the second neighbor waved them off. "Are you asking them and their empire to come to our village? What in the world are you thinking? Their empire is our enemy. I don't want their empire to come."

One of Jesus' companions smiled and said, "Don't worry. You'll see." And then all three of them shouted again: "Let your empire come," and then laughed.

By this time the neighbors' worst nightmare seemed to be materializing. One of the commanders and four other soldiers were headed straight for Jesus and his shouting companions. Just before the soldiers arrived, another group shout echoed off the houses.

The commander spoke in common Greek, "What are you doing?" Several of the villagers, looking puzzled, mumbled to each other in Aramaic. Quickly recalculating, he then mustered his best Aramaic to repeat the question: "What you doing? Shouting at soldiers not permitted."

"We are praying," answered Jesus. "This is our religious obligation."

Puzzled and not knowing whether to be insulted or not, the commander pursued the matter: "What you pray? Tell again your prayer."

Delighted at the invitation, Jesus and his friends shouted again, "Let your empire come."

"What you mean? We Rome are empire. What you mean, 'let your empire come?'" the commander retorted.

Jesus' friend answered with a broad knowing smile, "We are asking for God's empire to come. It is our religious obligation."

Still puzzled, but wanting to observe the Roman policy of religious tolerance, the commander sought clarification: "No Jerusalem empire? Just God empire?"

Jesus spoke up: "We give to Caesar what is Caesar's and to God what is God's. Prayer is to God."

Wanting to be certain no political intrigue was afoot, the commander made another mistake, now to the delight of all the neighbors: "Tell again what you pray."

Jesus looked around at the group of nine people now gathered around the soldiers, lifted his hands in the traditional prayer gesture, smiled at everyone, while all of the villagers present bellowed, "Let your empire come."

Still puzzled but somewhat assured by the resultant laughter of the villagers, the commander said, "Long live Caesar," turned, and left with the other soldiers. As they walked back to join the company, the villagers all raised their hands in prayer and shouted, "Let your empire come. Let your empire come. Amen. Amen."

Conclusion

Placing a prayer plea for the coming of God's "basileia" in the context of village life Jesus' Galilee makes sense of it as a prayer of Jesus. As noted earlier, the wide range of applications of the notion of "God's basileia" in the Jesus tradition certainly implies that Jesus could have prayed "Let your basileia come" in a variety of settings with a number of different effects. It is clear both from Jesus' teachings and from the pithiness of this prayer sentence that the prayer itself had many social edges. As a short prayer in an everday Galilean setting, it came alive just as Jesus' aphorisms did.

It is true that this prayer fragment could have acted as a summary of the Q resolve to stay the course in the search for wisdom. In such a case its originality would perhaps belong to the sages who followed Jesus. But the very strong possibility of Jesus praying "Let your basileia come" within specific contexts of his life, and not as a part of some larger "Lord's Prayer," is now very clear. With the many possible contexts for such a "basileia" prayer, the meaning of the various prayer fragments expands exponentially, and the picture of the aphoristic Jesus at prayer becomes more frameable.

8

Give Us the Bread
We Need for Today

Jesus and some of his followers wandered around the Galilean countryside, teaching and eating what was given them. Although in the generation after Jesus there are clear instructions for how to go about this
(don't carry much with you, beg when you need to, and get out of town
when you're not welcome), it is less clear exactly how Jesus did this.

One of Jesus' core sayings found in the Gospel of Thomas gives some
idea (14:4):

> When you go into any region and walk about in the countryside, when
> people take you in, eat what they serve you.

Luke 10:7 makes a similar impression:

> Stay at that one house, eating and drinking whatever they provide.

The lifestyle of wandering teachers who relied on the hospitality of
others was fairly well known in the eastern Mediterranean world.
Especially individuals who practiced popular Cynic philosophy had very
similar approaches to teaching and eating at other people's houses. So,
the likelihood that Jesus might beg for food and/or hope for a dinner invitation where he could do some teaching fits well into a larger pattern of
behavior in his part of the world.

As was imagined in the opening pages of this book, it is most likely in
this context that Jesus prayed: "Provide us with the bread we need for the
day." Since Jesus seemed to be dependent on others for his food—at least
while he was on the road teaching—such a prayer would have asked simply that he receive enough food for that day. In this regard, it is important
to note that the prayer sentence in Matthew is closer to the historical
Jesus than Luke. Luke has generalized this sentence into a request for food
day after day.

This simple sentence prayer is striking in the way it cast Jesus on the care of God, and freed him from dependence on the conventions of family or accumulated wealth. Jesus' prayer for only the current day's bread fits very well with his teachings. In Thom 36:1 we read:

> Don't fret from morning to evening and evening to morning about your food.

And in Luke 12:24, Jesus said,

> Think about the crows: they don't plant or harvest, they don't have storerooms or barns. Yet God feeds them.

So praying for bread just for today corresponds on two levels to Jesus' life as a sage:

1. It reflects the fact that Jesus was in need of food each day. The activity of being a sage did not provide him with a regular source of food, and when he was on the road, he did not know where he was sleeping or eating.

2. It corresponds to the wisdom Jesus was teaching: that one should not worry about the accumulation of food and drink, but simply let each day take care of itself. As the opening sketch in the book illustrates, Jesus and his companions seem purposely to have put themselves in positions where they did not know what they would eat the next day. Their prayer for bread just one day at a time was a part of their larger program of learning to depend on God's domain, not on the conventions of family, empire, temple, or marketplace.

As was suggested in the opening sketch of the book, Jesus praying for the bread he needed just for today should be seen in the context of a good deal of hunger in the Galilean peasantry. By this prayer he joined himself to the peasants' plight, spoke to his own immediate needs of finding something to sustain himself, and tweaked both himself and the peasants around him to trust more deeply in God.

In this setting this prayer fragment—not as a part of the "Lord's Prayer," but as a sentence said in the middle of the need for bread among the Galilean peasants and sages—makes a great deal of sense as a prayer of the historical Jesus. It becomes another example of the way the prayer fragments behind the Lord's Prayer are actually free-standing, pithy sentence prayers in specific social contexts. Just as the Abba, Your name be revered, and basileia prayer sentences stand on their own and match the contexts of both Jesus' Galilean situation and his aphoristic teaching style, this prayer for bread just for today begins to fill out a picture of Jesus at prayer.

9

Forgive Our Debts

"Forgive our debts to the extent that we have forgiven those in debt to us." (Matt 6:12) As we saw in chapter four, indebtedness was one of the major social and economic problems of first-century Israel. The peasant farmers and the merchants in the towns and villages were constantly in danger of falling into serious debt—often with the result of losing lands or businesses—to the landed class and to the urban elite. Although these cycles of indebtedness were acute in the first century, the peasant class of Israel during the previous twelve hundred years had rarely been out of danger of debt. This long history of indebtedness among the peasants probably had many of its roots in the less than ideal growing conditions in Israel, coupled with economic pressures from successful urban centers of commerce.

The core teachings of Jesus were very conscious of the realities of debt. A good number of sayings referred to persons in one stage or another of indebtedness (for example, Matt 18:23–24 and Luke 16:1–8). The parable of the shrewd manager who discounts debts owed to his master, Jesus' instructions about lending money, and the parable of the unforgiving slave all referred directly to the dilemmas of small merchants and peasant farmers who didn't have enough money.

Interestingly enough these sayings do not reveal a consistent attitude of Jesus toward the variety of problems related to indebtedness. They do show a strong awareness that the problem exists, but they seemed to resist consistently condemning either the debtor or the lender.

The sentence prayer "forgive our debts to the extent that we have forgiven those in debt to us" in Matt 6:12 addressed this critical socioeconomic problem in Israel. Later versions of the prayer (beginning with Luke's version of the Lord's Prayer) have made it into a prayer about the forgiveness of sins in general. But Matthew clearly referred to debts, not sins, and thus appears to preserve the version closest to the historical Jesus.

This sentence prayer asked God for relief from debt, not to be forgiven for sins. What an interesting double-take this occasions for pious Christians in our day, to imagine that Jesus was in debt, and that he prayed to God to be somehow released from this indebtedness!

But, as with many of the core sayings of Jesus, this prayer had a twist to it. It not only sought forgiveness of debts, but committed Jesus and his friends to write off whatever anyone owed them. In effect, the prayer asked God to cooperate in doing away with the entire system of indebtedness. In the process it pushed the one praying and those listening to consider releasing their neighbors from any debts they might have.

This fits with the only other direct teaching we have from the historical Jesus about the subject. In Thom 95:1–2, Jesus instructs:

> If you have money, don't lend it at interest. Rather give it to someone from whom you won't get it back.

Jesus Prays About Debt

Another sketch of the Galilean context for this sentence prayer of Jesus may help overcome the initial sense of oddness upon reading a prayer about indebtedness.

A STORY

Like many unattached women of his day, Jesus' mother was very vulnerable financially. When Jesus and his brother were teenagers, she had been forced to sell her house so that they could have enough to eat and to clothe themselves. They had then moved in with neighbors to whom they paid varying combinations of money and labor. That relationship continued to be good.

Although Jesus' brother was now working as a fisherman, Jesus' sage vocation provided no money at all. Indeed the last time Mary and her other son had seen Jesus, he had shown little interest in them at all. Jesus' brother and mother had in the meantime been forced to borrow money from the fabric merchant in Nazareth, and Mary's host family was in danger of losing their house because of their own indebtedness. It was also true that a cousin of Mary's still owed her a decent sum of money from years ago, but that cousin was quite ill.

So when Jesus came home to Nazareth this time, the pressure was on almost everyone. Jesus and his brother were angry. They hated the thought that their mother was once again close to homelessness. Both had traveled enough to know that the combination of Roman rule, bad crops, and greedy landowners from the city were root causes of their mother's precarious situation.

That evening Jesus, his brother, Mary, and her host family were all sitting on the ground in front of the house. There was enough of a chill in the air that the small fire around which they gathered felt comforting. Yet there was strain in the air, as everyone's imagination labored to see a future for Mary and her host family.

Jesus began to cry quietly. Seeking comfort, Mary reached her hand out to her other son. The others occasionally chatted with one another.

Below Jesus' soft sobs, his voice awoke. The words were slow and steady. "Forgive ... Forgive us ... Forgive us our debts ... our debts." His prayer hung in the brisk evening air. The others had fallen silent. "Forgive us ... our debts ... to the extent we have ... Forgiven those in debt to us." Jesus' brother thought of all the fishermen he knew who were struggling to feed their families. Mary thought of her cousin who owed her money. Jesus' prayer hovered over them all, as their bondedness to one another and to so many others tugged at their insides.

Conclusions

Situating this sentence prayer within its social context makes clear that it arose from certain specific situations in which Jesus found himself. It did not,within the lifetime of Jesus, belong to the Lord's Prayer, which was the product of the generations after Jesus. As we have seen in chapter four, after Jesus was gone, his followers in Galilee formulated a general prayer in his name, combining fragments from Jesus' own prayers with other material to create an institutionalized prayer in Jesus' name. As the various versions of this Lord's Prayer from the second half of the first century were passed on, the meanings of the individual prayer sentences were generalized and taken out of context. The sentence prayer about forgiveness made a gradual transition from forgiving one another's debts to forgiveness of sins.

In the context of Jesus' life as a sage in Galilee this prayer fragment was both a dramatic address to a major social problem of his time, and yet another clever tweak to engage those around him in a new level of awareness about their responsibilities relative to the vexing problem of indebtedness.

This final prayer fragment from beneath the Q Jesus Prayer complements the other fragments in that they all spring to life as independent prayers within Jesus' social context and teaching style. We are now in a position to ask what they tell us about Jesus at prayer.

10

The Pieces Fit Together

A NEW BIG PICTURE
OF JESUS AT PRAYER

Reviewing the five prayer fragments which seem to belong to the historical Jesus has transformed them. Rather than just five simple or partial sentences, they have become a rather astounding kind of prayer.

The pieces really do fit together. As the individual prayer fragments have been carefully placed within life situations of the historical Jesus, the prayers have sprung to life. They end up being highly involved in fresh and gutsy ways with the Galilean people and the society in which Jesus lived.

Granted, it was an unusual prayer life. One that does not look much like the way we pray today. Nor like the way our grandmothers prayed. Nor like the way most of the current spirituality movements are encouraging us to pray. It was probably not so unusual in Jesus' day, although his wit certainly made it some of the best of its kind.

It was a prayer life that kept its edge. Each of the five fragments, seen anew in its restored setting, revealed a Jesus whose prayer life did not let anyone off easy. Speaking to God in new colloquial language, dealing with family pressure and imperial tyranny, pressing himself and others to risk, insisting on self-awareness—these challenges created an intensity that gave off sparks.

The pieces also fit the picture of the historical Jesus emerging from twentieth century scholarship. These sentence prayers sound astonishingly like Jesus' parables and his beatitudes. The prayer life of Jesus this study has painstakingly uncovered is of a piece with the rest of his teaching.

This, of course, is both a great relief and quite shocking for the conventional Christian imagination. It is a relief, because the historical Jesus does not end up being some bizarre composite of all of the gospel portraits of him. It is no longer necessary to assign to him both the grandiose prayers in John and the almost secretive prayers in Matthew. From the point of view of his prayers this reconstruction of historical Jesus makes him look human, sane and brilliant.

On the other hand, the fact that the prayer life of Jesus uncovered in this study fits with his early teachings challenges conventional Christian pictures of him. His prayers make such good sense alongside of his teachings that we no longer need to resort to claiming some divine-human split to explain his actions and his prayers. He looks like a regular—and very talented—human being, who prayed in ways similar to his teaching. This portrait, however, calls many pious pictures of Jesus into question. Along with the re-assurance of a coherent picture of the historical Jesus comes the disturbing recognition that the conventional pictures of him entreating his Father that all might be one or teaching his disciples a prayer to be repeated are much less credible historically.

In the next chapters, then, we can proceed to cash in on our rigorous study of all the references to Jesus praying. The way these fragments have come back together will help us understand the general principles of Jesus' prayer life, and we shall see what he has to teach us about how we pray.

11
What Jesus Prayed About

Was prayer a large part of Jesus' life? What did he pray about? In what kind of situations would one have found Jesus praying?

We can now step back and ask some larger questions about the character of Jesus' prayer life. The detailed analysis of first century texts and contexts undertaken in the last seven chapters point toward some major conclusions concerning where and how much Jesus prayed.

Having sorted out a range of material that is historically unreliable, and having discovered important prayer fragments within the early versions of the Lord's Prayer, we have a standpoint from which to assess what the focal points of Jesus' prayer life were. In particular, understanding that the separate fragments of the Lord's Prayer make sense in the life of the Galilean sage (as shown in chaps. 5 through 9) can point us toward an overview of what Jesus prayed about.

Business

Jesus prayed about money and money problems. These prayers concerned both his own personal economic situation and the bigger economic problems of his society.

Jesus' prayer about debts was clearly a personal plea that he , his neighbors, and his friends could be free from indebtedness. Yet it was a two-edged challenge which involved both a request for relief and a self-examination about the responsibility of the one indebted.

Jesus' prayer asking for the basileia of God to come almost certainly sprang from the economic injustice of his situation. Jesus' teaching, "Blessed are the poor, for the reign of God belongs to them," indicated that when he thought of the basileia/reign of God, it was at least partly in terms of the economic plight of the people around him.

Politics

Given the obvious parody on the Roman empire which is a part of
Jesus' prayer and teachings about the basileia/empire of God, it is clear
that Jesus' prayer life was full of political controversy and aspirations.
When Jesus prayed "Let your basileia/empire come," it was to many ears
a direct insult to the Roman basileia/empire.

Uttered in the presence of Roman soldiers, such a prayer could have
gotten him in immediate trouble. Even invoking God's empire in the
market square or at a meal would incorporate the political opposition of
Galilean Jews into a prayer.

Sex

Jesus actively contrasted God's basileia to men proud of their ability to
conceive children in his saying, "There are castrated men who castrated
themselves because of Heaven's imperial rule" (Matt 19:12). Here Jesus
challenged the pride of men able to produce children by tweaking them
with the image of men castrating themselves for the cause of God's
basileia/domain.

So when he prayed "Let your basileia come," he most likely also
thought about it in terms of sex. It is easy to picture Jesus praying such a
prayer both as a request for relief from the arrogant fixation on male sexual production and (for those with ears to hear) as a challenge to others
to re-examine their way of thinking about themselves.

Religion

That Jesus prayed made him a religious person. But it is also fairly clear
that he prayed about religious matters. Although some recent portraits of
Jesus have made him uninterested in any religious questions, our prayer
fragments often show him praying about religious matters in a rather
funny manner.

For example, by employing the combined prayer fragment "Abba, your
name be revered," he was actively reflecting on the question of God's
holiness and re-working a traditional prayer from the Eighteen
Benedictions. As noted in chapter six, this clever formulation challenged
the normal notions of God's holiness by associating God's holy name
with the ordinary word for father, "Abba." By using conventional religious terms and in prayer re-casting them, he was trying to re-frame what
was holy to include the most ordinary parts of life.

Family

As we have seen in chapter five, when Jesus prayed "Abba," his prayer was placing him in the middle of a larger mix of family politics. Calling God "Abba/Father" was not usual. Loyalty to one's own Abba/father and depending on one's own father-led family was the primary reality people thought of when they heard "Abba." Calling God "Abba" in prayer challenged the conventional family dependence on fathers and family loyalty, and cast the one praying on the care of someone much more intangible.

This prayer challenge to the family fit within the larger set of teachings by the historical Jesus, who actively questioned, "My mother and my brothers—whoever are they? ... Here are my mother and my brothers. For whoever does the will of my Father in heaven, that's my brother and sister and mother" (Matt 12:48–50).

On the Road

The sage Jesus, like many others like him in the ancient Mediterranean, walked from village to village without belongings and asked for shelter and food in exchange for his wisdom. This meant that he was quite vulnerable to the elements, and even more vulnerable than most Galilean peasants to hunger.

From our examination of the prayer fragment "Give us the bread we need for today," it is clear that Jesus prayed about this vulnerability. This prayer was almost certainly prayed while Jesus was on the road and without any assurance of food. As chapter eight detailed, this prayer was not just a plea for food, but also a challenge to the one praying not to think about tomorrow's needs, but to stay present to the moment.

In a way this prayer on the road is a fairly close equivalent to praying on the job today. For Jesus going on the road without any assurance of food was part of his sage job description. This prayer fragment illustrated his praying while working.

Education

Jesus' quest for wisdom seemed to have been all-consuming. He trusted that "everything hidden could be uncovered." He encouraged others to experience the hidden care of God available when one uncovered the pretense of superficial securities.

Like other sages, Jesus seemed to know that the wisdom present all around him gave him a certain freedom. This made him aware that those who thought they ruled—the Romans, the temple authorities, the family authorities, the wealthy—really were not in charge. The liberating wisdom these sages discovered pointed them toward their participation in the intangible reign of God.

So when Jesus prayed "Let your basileia/reign come," this prayer was said within the context of his larger quest for and assurance of wisdom in all things. In this sense, Jesus' invocation of God's reign was a sage's way of renewing his devotion to wisdom itself. It was yet another way of Jesus casting himself on the intangible net of care that wisdom provided. In this sense "Let your basileia/reign come" must have been uttered by Jesus just at the moments when his search for wisdom was most tensive and uncertain. It was a way of saying "yes" to the task of opening himself to the wisdom yet to be learned—so close at hand, yet so hidden.

Conclusion

There is no way of determining how frequently Jesus prayed. The picture Luke painted of Jesus praying at every important juncture in his life has unfortunately proven unreliable historically.

However, the large range of life issues evoked by the prayer fragments in this chapter's review indicates that he prayed in a wide variety of settings about a broad spectrum of issues. It seems likely then that Jesus prayed often and in many different places. In fact, his prayer life seems to have been much more broadly focused than that of many religious people today. The contemporary taboos about prayers concerning sex, business, and politics were almost certainly not in effect in Jesus' prayer life.

In addition, Jesus' curiously interactive style of prayer (to be discussed in detail in the next chapter) must have led him to pray frequently in public and in situations where people were surprised by the fact that he was praying and they were listening.

12

How Jesus Prayed

In some ways the prayer life of Jesus, the clever and hopeful sage, could not have been anything else than what we have discovered. His way of praying seems to have sprung directly from his general sense of himself as a sage.

He prayed as one who was, in the finest sense, an educator. The Latin roots for our word "education" mean "to draw out." An educator in this sense draws learning out of the student, rather than pouring information in. Jesus' prayer life drew people out. In a surprising turn of events, we have discovered a style of prayer in Jesus that is very akin to his style as a wisdom teacher.

Just as his short parables and sayings surprised people and helped them look at their families, their belonging to the Roman empire, their economic situation, and their Jewish piety in new ways, so Jesus' prayer did the same thing. As has been noted, his prayer about indebtedness began as a plea, but ended as an internal call to self-examination. When hungry, he prayed for bread in such a way as to make people laugh and cast themselves on God's care with a new kind of freedom. In his prayer, he demanded a great deal of himself and of those who were listening or praying along.

Going behind the Lord's Prayer to discover the prayer fragments of Jesus has produced a more unified profile of Jesus. The prayer fragments show a Jesus at prayer who is consistent with Jesus the aphoristic sage, someone who challenged both convention and himself. It has for quite some time been a conceptual problem for scholars to reconcile the iconoclastic character of Jesus' parables, aphorisms, and radical behavioral proposals with a Lord's Prayer meant for repeating—or even a Lord's Prayer that catalogued a series of Jesus' concerns. As the review of prayer fragments in chapters 5 through 9 has illustrated, breaking the individual segments into smaller unconnected units re-connects them with the earliest sayings of Jesus the sage.

Since aphorists and iconoclasts of our day are not much given to prayer, it has been difficult to associate prayer with the kind of teaching reflected in the core sayings of Jesus. But that was not the case in either the Jewish or non-Jewish wisdom traditions. As Gerald Downing notes, there are numerous examples of God being "thanked and praised, trusted, addressed and referred to as Father, God of all, guiding and enlightening individuals for the general good, always forgiving, despite the evident wickedness of humanity" by non-Jewish Mediterranean sages (*Cynics and Christian Origins*, 135). The extensive prayer in the first-century Wisdom of Solomon 9:1–18 is a dramatic example of Jewish wisdom merging the themes of learning and God's reign. Even though contemporary aphorists do not pray much, Jesus the sage stood in an active tradition of prayer.

How then did that particular tradition of prayer contribute to the practice of the historical Jesus?

Jesus' Prayers Made People React

Jesus' particular "style" of prayer as evidenced in these fragments involved intense interaction with the people around him. Although he most probably employed some rote prayer during his life time (e.g. "Your name be revered"), most of the prayer fragments seem to suggest he was highly conscious of people listening in—either in actuality or by their psychological presence in Jesus' mind.

The way he used "Abba," and "Abba, your name be revered," seems to have almost required someone listening and reacting either with something like "You can't talk about God that way" or with an understanding chuckle. Part of the power of the prayer seems to have resided in the reaction of those around Jesus. Similarly chapters 7 and 11's survey of possible meanings of "Let your basileia come" propelled us into seeing Jesus using this prayer in front of Roman soldiers, with a group of men bragging about their sexual prowess, among sages trying to learn some more, at banquets or in markets. "Forgive us our debts to the extent that we forgive those indebted to us" would have had much more power when prayed in the company of other debtors. As we saw in the book's opening pages, "Give us the bread we need for today" so radically incorporates the (human) listeners' responses that the prayer itself was in large part defined by the interaction between Jesus and those people who were listening.

I do not mean to suggest any hypocrisy on Jesus' part. For many people

today prayer that is conscious of others' listening in is considered hypocritical, because it is not focusing exclusively on God. In view of the consistent tendency of Jesus' prayers to have been very conscious of people
listening, I suggest that such prayer could have had its own (very different) integrity in the very fact of its being evocatively socially interactive.
In this sense the engagement with God in prayer did not in any way
exclude simultaneous interaction with people.

As we come to see the intensely social character of Jesus' prayer, we
come to recognize that it promotes both creativity and vulnerability. To
assert one's own obligation to forgive debts as a condition for one's own
release from this aspect of crushing poverty—all while praying—was self-
criticism in the presence of both God and those listening. By first evok-
ing the general hope of release from debt and then surprising everyone
with the assertion of mutual release from indebtedness, the prayer trig-
gered in the worst case an angry glare, in the best an appreciative smile.

Of course, the same dynamic was obvious in the prayers about bread,
Abba, the reverence of God's name, and perhaps the coming of God's
basileia. In each case both the one praying and those listening found
themselves exposed.

This kind of social vulnerability in prayer must have opened up those
listening. Everyone in such a situation had to have decided in the midst
of the prayer event to close down and escape or open more deeply to one
another and to God.

In this way the intensely social character of Jesus' prayer life called
forth a kind of corporate embodiedness not common in contemporary
prayer practices (with the possible exception of twentieth century charismatic movements). Jesus' prayer seemed to have been as much directed at
his listeners as at God. Purposefully aware of the reactions his prayer
would produce, he impelled others to a new level of group consciousness.
Suddenly those listening to or praying with him were aware that they
were indebted or obliged to one another in new ways, at one with one
another in their need for bread and spontaneity, and with new eyes for the
creative reign of God.

Jesus' Prayers Helped People Learn

Another way of thinking about this style of prayer derives from the
teaching character of Jesus' activity. Prayers which delight in interaction
with others (such as the ones we have discovered beneath the Lord's
Prayer) fit quite easily into the mentality of an aphoristic teacher. Indeed,

one could say that the aphoristic teacher Jesus brought that teaching/learning dynamic to his prayer. He does not seem to have been able to turn off the teacher/learner interaction in his prayer. That there was nothing hidden which could not be discovered characterized the way Jesus prayed. These prayer fragments thrived on exposing the one praying and those listening. When Jesus prayed this way, his prayer opened him up to learning something new. Prayer and learning merged as his address to God became the occasion for seeing himself in a new and larger picture. Similarly his prayer challenged those listening to have what was hidden uncovered. Praying for bread just for today or revering the ordinary name of Abba as divine pushed those listening to his prayer to look at and learn about that new and larger picture.

By associating Jesus' prayer with his teaching, I do not mean to suggest that Jesus taught prayers. Gerald Downing's summary of sages at prayer seems to make best sense of the way Jesus' teaching and praying mixed. Downing notes that the Jewish and non-Jewish sages alike were not at all shy in praying, but were equally insistent that prayers not be taught (*Cynics and Christian Origins*, 133–35). Jesus as an aphoristic sage employed evocative and socially interactive prayers that taught implicitly, as aphorisms do. But this style of teaching intended to draw responses from within the persons listening, not to invite rote repetition. The prayers of Jesus—like the sayings—were often striking enough, however, to be remembered, elaborated, and probably mimicked. This memorable clever quality to the prayers explains why the prayer fragments were remembered and eventually repeated by Jesus' followers.

Did Jesus Pray Alone?

This highly socially interactive style of prayer stands in some contrast to the gospel portraits of Jesus alone in prayer. As shown in chapter two the gospel portraits of Jesus alone at prayer seem to be the product of the gospel writers,and as such were voted historically unreliable by the Jesus Seminar. There are, however, some contemporary scholars, including Jesus Seminar member Marcus Borg who have insisted that the historical Jesus often prayed alone. It is, of course, not impossible that he used both styles of prayer. He could have prayed alone, even though there are no reliable texts supporting such a picture. The fairest conclusion seems to be that we have no credible evidence to say that he did or did not pray alone.

One can speculate that Jesus prayed alone. Since the prayer fragments close to the historical Jesus reflect such a deep level of self-consciousness, it is easy to note that most people today at least would need some time alone to think through such formulations. Such a self-critical style of prayer as is evident in these prayer fragments would have been easily companioned by intense time alone, at least in contemporary western peoples' minds. The devotion to wisdom of ancient near eastern sages like Jesus, as many scholars have noted, was as much about some kind of silent search as about expressing short tricky sayings. So there are a number of ways of speculating that Jesus prayed alone a great deal.

I would express two major cautions, however, about giving too much license to such speculation. They are:

1. There does not seem to be any reliable textual evidence that Jesus prayed alone to any substantial degree. On the contrary, all the textual evidence this book has been able to excavate points to an intensely social kind of prayer. Any sustained case for the historical reliability of Jesus praying alone to any extent needs some support from the first century documents.

2. The tendency to push this speculation so far that Jesus' public prayer life is necessarily rooted in solitary prayer diminishes our appreciation of the intensely social style of prayer which has emerged with such surprising consistency from the basic prayer texts of the historical Jesus.

Did Jesus Pray Traditional Prayers?

That we have found in Jesus' own prayer fragments a direct quotation from the Eighteen Benedictions, a traditional daily Jewish liturgical prayer, is strong support for the notion of Jesus praying traditional Jewish prayers. This direct connection between "Your name be revered" (Holy be your name) and traditional Jewish material reinforces a common sense observation that as a Galilean Jew, Jesus almost certainly prayed those traditional sentences. From this it can be deduced that Jesus at a number of points in his life prayed traditional Jewish prayers in his home, in the homes of others, and—if there were synagogues in Galilee in the first third of the first century (a matter of much scholarly debate and little archeological support)—in the synagogues.

In the combined prayer fragment, "Abba, your name be revered," there was, however, a definite intention to subvert and transform the meaning of a traditional Jewish prayer. So while being relatively certain that in his lifetime Jesus prayed traditional Jewish prayers, we cannot tell what role they played in his life, especially during his life as a sage. One can imagine fairly easily how "Abba, your name is holy" could have been a challenging, humor-filled, and evocative part of the eighteen benedictions said in the home of one whose piety was cast in a traditional mold. Certainly Jesus had the boldness to combine prayer and humor. His unorthodox references to women, yeast, poor people, and defecation (all at one level or another offensive to his listeners) showed this kind of nerve.

Although there is not enough evidence either for Jesus' thorough and on-going participation in traditional Jewish prayer or for his rejection of it, I suspect that he did continue to use a fair amount of traditional Jewish prayer, while also actively undermining, cajoling, and remaking those same prayers in the service of the uncovering of God's wisdom. Although on points such a these, the slim textual support available makes for little more than speculation, it is quite possible that until his death Jesus both actively subverted and participated in traditional Jewish prayer.

Conclusion

The only historically reliable texts about Jesus' prayer life point toward an intensely socially interactive, highly self-critical, and deftly educational style of prayer. These texts, when placed in their first century contexts and alongside one another, have uncovered a style of prayer strikingly different from Jewish or Christian liturgical material, Protestant prayer meetings, pastoral prayers, charismatic ecstasy, Roman Catholic hours of prayer, new age impulses, and mystical meditations. There are no historically reliable texts about Jesus praying in seclusion and only one comically complicated text in which Jesus employs (and puts a wry spin on) traditional Jewish prayer.

As discussed above in the section on Jesus praying alone, this does not mean that one cannot imagine Jesus being a mystic, praying often in seclusion, organizing pietistic prayer meetings, chanting a new age mantra, or praying liturgically with others. But such imaginings—as inviting as they might be—carry with them the major danger of turning Jesus' prayer life back into what we wish it had been. Such domestication of Jesus' fresh and different kind of prayer all too easily dismisses the insights our textual rigors have uncovered. In our prosaic, historical exercise we have stumbled upon a very different style of prayer in the earliest Jesus texts. It is in fact so different, that as will be noted in the chapter to come, it is difficult for us today to think of learning from it.

Rather than immediately try to associate this style with familiar contemporary prayer styles, why not stay present to the newness of its intense social interaction and its exaggerated degree of self-consciousness? No harm is done in considering such a different style of prayer. Perhaps it might teach us something, as we open ourselves to it. It is to that hope we now turn.

13

How We Pray Today

IMPLICATIONS FROM
THE HISTORICAL JESUS

Can we learn from the curious, sage-like prayer life of the historical Jesus? What implications does his style of prayer have for the development of spirituality in our day?

Jesus' prayer life was very different from almost anything we see in spirituality today. This was so not so much because he was divine or a completely exceptional human being, but because he belonged to an energized wisdom movement unlike almost anything that exists in our day. So on one level we must say that even if the historical Jesus' prayer life seems attractive (it may not to some), it is almost impossible to imitate because we are not a part of a group of wise-cracking, risk-taking, hope-filled sages.

On the other hand, there are dimensions to Jesus' prayer life from which we might learn and profit today. These elements include intense socially interactive prayer, highly self-critical prayer, prayer life "on the run" set in the hustle and bustle of daily life, and prayer linked to learning.

Socially Interactive Prayer

Jesus' prayer life was intensely interactive to the point that it is difficult for most people today to conceive of it. How can one pray to God, be self-critical, and challenge one's listeners all at the same time? Surely doing all of this at the same time would make most of us today either distracted or so hopelessly self-conscious as to rule out awareness of God. Yet, from the ways Jesus' prayer fragments have been shown to interact with particular social settings, it is clear that in these bits of prayer we have an extraordinarily complex human consciousness. It was a consciousness that one cannot attribute simplistically to some notion of Jesus' unique divinity, since the consciousness belonged to very specific socioeconomic and cultural patterns of village life in first century Galilee. It was most likely a consciousness produced by the synergy of near eastern sages working together for centuries and the peculiarities of Jesus' own life. Still—as difficult as it may seem today—it is a consciousness we today might learn from in prayer.

Jesus' prayer life made him extremely vulnerable to others. His openness to other people in these prayer fragments seems inseparable from his openness to God. This poses the question to those praying today: can they learn to be similarly open and vulnerable to others as they pray? Because of this openness Jesus' prayer calls forth the possibility of a new kind of social body in prayer, in which individual transcendence of their own self-consciousness unites them in a way that they are both open to one another and encouraged in their own self-criticism.

It looks as if Jesus' intensely socially interactive prayer did not customarily occur in organized prayer sessions. Rather, Jesus seems to have surprised people in groups with short, quirky prayers that caught them off guard. We can only begin to imagine how to pray like this. What would it be like to pray in the middle of a secular situation in ways that made people laugh, get angry, and/or think twice? I know of no contemporary example, although I find myself delighted with the possibility.

The one place where a similar kind of more domesticated social interaction might happen with some regularity today is in organized liturgical or worship settings. There is—emerging within many liberal Christian congregations and as a part of on-going charismatic groups—a certain style of organized prayer where spontaneous individual prayers engage the whole group in reflection. These prayers, which often take the form of thanksgiving or asking for help, effectively form bonds among those praying even as the people pray to God.

Self-critical Prayer

The degree to which Jesus' prayer life was self-questioning and self-challenging has proved astounding. The way his prayer for bread forced the issue of eating "whatever is provided" pushed him to even higher willingness to live in the moment. The manner in which his prayer for release from debts made him responsible for justice was highly self-critical.

Perhaps most remarkable has been the emerging scenario in which Jesus seems to have made the taunts he may have experienced as a fatherless child into a matter of self-examination in public. It appears very possible that Jesus took the public mockery of his own fatherlessness, and—by crying out to God as father—opened himself to further ridicule, while searching in an intensely public manner for God's fatherly care. In his

"Abba" prayer, Jesus challenged himself to claim his own fatherlessness and—through openness—to transform it into an experience of God.

This kind of self-criticism in prayer has obvious potential for personal growth. Opening one's self to criticism as one prays (especially publicly) promises to unblock many impediments to the receptivity of truth and beauty.

The contemporary prayer movement of spiritual direction, in which an individual opens her/himself to God and to a spiritual director in a regularly monthly session, has potential for this same kind of self-criticism in prayer. Here the dialogue with the spiritual director can allow for the one praying to call him/herself into question in ways that greatly promote a deeper relationship with God and to personal growth.

Similar dynamics can occur in pastoral counseling, in small prayer groups, and in various kinds of therapy. It is not accidental that many secular therapists today are seeking way to integrate spiritual practice into counseling sessions.

The limitations in spiritual direction, counseling, and various small groups relative to Jesus' self-critical style of prayer are obvious. Jesus seems to have made himself vulnerable to such criticism in a fairly public manner, while all of these contemporary movements are characterized by their protectedness and intimacy. Similarly, Jesus encouraged self-criticism in his prayers concerning social and political matters (e.g. indebtedness), not just the highly personal subject matter of most spiritual direction, prayer groups, and counseling.

Prayer on the Run

Jesus' prayer, as manifested in the fragments, was consistently injected into real life events. He prayed about holiness while challenging people's dependency on family loyalties. He asked for God's basileia/domain to come in relationship to people's sex life, their political allegiances, and their business. Even more to the point, the prayers seem to have always been said with the expectation that there were people around to respond to the prayer.

This raises not only the issue of the social interactiveness of Jesus-style prayer (addressed earlier in this chapter), but also whether one can pray in the middle of life's busy-ness. Such prayer does not seem to need any special holy setting. It happens almost spontaneously in the middle of life. The character of this prayer in the middle of the busy workday, however, is usually not just the occasional plea for help, when one runs into trouble. It seems much more like an intensification of one's own social awareness and self-criticism in the middle of crucial events that happen in the daily course of events.

But even when one cannot consciously intensify one's awareness in the midst of a particular event, a first step could include praying as a part of daily routines. Praying while the computer boots up or while access to the internet occurs, or while waiting in a car at a stoplight, or standing in line— any and all of these might be occasions for this on-the-run prayer style.

Prayer Life Linked to Learning Today

Jesus' quest for learning was linked to his prayer life primarily through the way wisdom helped him understand the character of God's basileia/reign. Although academics and spirituality in our culture have generally been separated, Jesus' example raises the possibility of education being a primary element in the way one prays.

Perhaps most true to Jesus' combintation of prayer and learning would be an integration of important conversation with prayer. Imagine following Jesus' example by praying aloud spontaneously in the middle of an important conversation. In Jesus' style this would certainly be a prayer spoken out loud in the middle of such a conversation. Or, if that kind of consciousness and boldness is not available to someone today, at least a silent prayer in the middle of a conversation in which one is actively learning could be very evocative. What if one might pray (silently or out loud) in the middle of a conversation about AIDS, "God, help me understand the cost and benefits of sex and intimacy." Or in the middle of a conversation about one's grandmother's hard life, a prayer like "Thank you, God, for her spunk."

This kind of prayer in the middle of conversation may be too demanding a way to begin integrating learning and prayer. A more basic way of doing something similar, yet still in the style of Jesus' search for wisdom, might be simply to pause during reading or during the watching of an informative TV show to pray one's anxiety, one's pain, or one's thanksgiving.

What We Pray For

It is, of course, not just how Jesus prayed that is evocative. It is also what he prayed about. The subject matter itself of Jesus' prayer life challenges us in a number of ways.

Breaking language barriers

Understanding that the historical Jesus prayed from time to time to God as "Abba/Father" points today to the need for similarly innovative prayer and God language that challenges old social patterns and fashions new human identity. Ironically the current experimentation of addressing God as "Mother" in prayer captures more of the spirit of Jesus at prayer than rote repetition of the now hyper-conventional prayers to God the Father. Praying to God as Mother today creates social challenges and personal reorientations very similar to those made by Jesus when he prayed the unconventional "Abba/Father."

It is not only in the area of inclusive language that language barriers need to be broken in prayer today. Too often people feel that they need to pray in pious sounding words and tones. This stands in explicit tension with Jesus' using common language such as "Abba" for his prayers. To the degree we are able to pray using ordinary speech instead of a manufactured religious language, some of the freshness of Jesus' own prayer may come forth.

As a matter of fact, the last fifty years have seen the emergence of a new energy to employ creative and poetic image-filled language in prayer. The power of poetry to use images can often break through barriers to another level of awareness. And learning this prayer style need not be daunting, for in addition to praying images from one's own life one can take advantage of the many new books in past fifty years which contain new, highly poetic prayers for many different life occasions.

The intersection of prayer and economic life style

The way Jesus' "Abba/Father" evoked a new trust in God over against dependence on social conventions clearly calls today for people to examine their reliance on material wealth, professional status, and social privilege, and the degree to which it stands in the way of a more open and trusting personal stance. For instance, for persons today to reject their car or credit card and begin proclaiming that God is their "car" or "credit card" would probably call forth responses similar to the ones Jesus encountered. Today to cast one's self on an invisible net of care outside the conventions of car or credit card would also be a window into a new experience of the divine.

In terms of prayer itself today, this suggests two moves:

1. Instead of fixating on the accumulation of wealth and security, people could spend more time casting themselves on God's intangible care.

Stopping to stare at a flower and take in its beauty, rather than working for the buying power to purchase more flowers, fits well with this style of prayer.

2. Praying about one's anxieties concerning security and wealth makes a great deal of sense within this perspective. The prayers of today's Americans treat one's economic status and money habits as inappropriate subject matter. Not so with the prayers of Jesus.

Prayer that extends the boundaries of the holy

Much of today's society also places artificial boundaries around what is reverenced or considered holy. People who wear clerical robes, use special kinds of vocabulary—whether that of the TV evangelist or the Pope—or assume pious postures claim or are presumed to have special access to holiness and God. Prayer itself in contemporary imagination is associated with the hushed tones and marks of reverence. The spirit of "Abba/Father, your name be revered" challenges these artificial boundaries.

To accomplish a similar opening up of contemporary imagination for the holy, a new and similarly shocking prayer would be necessary. Would an inner city prayer like "Homeboy, your turf is everywhere" have a similar effect to the Abba holiness prayer? Or, would the feminist spirituality of "Great Mother of all, your womb holds everything" make people smile and rethink the boundaries of holiness in similar ways? Or, since Jesus almost certainly prayed "Your name be revered" as a part of conventional piety, would a wild combination of popular piety and secular reference from today like "Amazing Grace, how sweet your kiss" evoke the hilarious combination of Abba/Father and the traditional honoring of God's name?

In any case, a keen sense of humor combined with a vivid, secular imagination is required in order to do justice to the comical and scandalous pairing of "Abba/Father" and "your name be revered."

Praying for God's rule

It is not difficult to see how the challenge of God's domain according to Jesus confronts contemporary society. God's reign, he would insist, challenges western materialism and the massive accumulation of wealth in our day. And now as then God's domain is probably best experienced with the birds of the air, the flowers of the field, the poor, and the children.

As in the first century, so also today God's imperial rule stands in strange juxtaposition to the ruling powers of the age. The phrase "imperial rule" evoked the domination of Rome in the first century. Today it is certainly American materialism, social values, and the spirit of free enterprise that dominate and corrupt. To pray for God's imperial rule to appear like leaven in bread and children at play is to long for another empire than the one in place.

A strange kind of practice developed in the religious social activism of the 1960s and 1970s in which people were encouraged to work for social justice and peace in the name of Jesus, but did not do much praying about it. Although there is no reason to compromise in any way the call to social justice and peace in the name of Jesus, the idea of praying about these goals, while actively promoting or patiently awaiting their eventual achievement, has considerable merit.

Praying for the bread we need

A lifestyle in which one only cares for the present day's food stands in stark contrast to the American way of life, where refrigerators and cupboards in most households are filled with foods from around the world. The sentence prayer of Jesus for just enough bread for today clashes almost obscenely with the traditional mildly self-congratulatory prayers in which Americans express thanks for the great bounty of the dinner table.

The American addiction to large amounts of food and an affluent lifestyle is far from the carefree, open-hearted attitude of the historical Jesus. Today individual identity and psychological survival are regularly bound up with possession of televisions, houses, automobiles, computers, credit cards, and attractive clothing. The focus on these possessions robs people of the potential to grow in trust and openness. Oddly enough, American society has enslaved both the affluent and the poor with its vision of material bounty.

What would happen if persons would begin their day with the prayer: "Just give me enough bread for the next twenty-four hours"? Wouldn't this increase the chances that people would spend more time building caring relationships, writing beautiful poetry, dancing in the moonlight, and working for justice?

Insofar as people become serious about breaking their materialist addictions in order to make space for the more spiritual dimensions of life, prayer can help in another area. Contemporary addictions to possessions and consumption are often partly due to repressed anxieties or painful experiences. Often people who have experienced difficult and painful situations will try to cover up their pain with material possessions. In these cases praying one's pain can help reduce the addiction to materialism. If one can feel one's pain and give it on to God, the need to cover up the memory of the pain decreases, and the possibility of living more spiritually comes closer.

Prayer and business

The prayer of Jesus about forgiving one another's debts raises a pointed question about doing business in today's world. It is difficult for most modern persons to consider seriously praying about the way they do business. At most, people today connect prayer and business by asking God for success.

But Jesus' prayer can be an occasion for re-evaluation and reflection on how we behave economically. This prayer challenges us to place our personal and/or corporate business in the context of God. It proposes that we apply God's standard of fairness and generosity to our own finances. In the American free enterprise economy, this runs counter to the assumption that we should and can do anything to make more money. Jesus' prayer about debts could be a model for how we today should pray about our tax forms, our employee benefits packages, our monthly bills, and our desires for raises.

Another way of learning something important from Jesus' prayer about indebtedness would be to take the catastrophic indebtedness of African, Asian, and Latin American nations into one's prayer life. That such indebtedness continues to be one of the major factors in the struggles of millions of Africans, Asians, and Latin Americans—perhaps a third of the people living on the planet—is surely a legitimate matter for prayer.

Like Jesus' prayer, such prayer would begin by asking for the end of indebtedness for these millions of people and scores of nations. But in the spirit of the self-critical and social character of Jesus' prayer, such prayer would also raise questions about the way Americans benefit from the indebtedness of these people. A prayer like "Forgive the debts of the African peoples insofar as I pay the real price for the coffee and tea I drink every morning" would capture that spirit.

Praying Beyond Jesus

Jesus' prayer life promises much to those who want to learn to pray in a way that supports and transforms the person praying. This chapter has outlined a number of healthy challenges his prayer presents. It becomes clear as we review his style and content of praying that depth and renewal await those who would follow him. Indeed the extraordinary levels of self-criticism, social presence, and learning exhibited in Jesus' prayers indicate that current styles of praying have a long way to go to catch up.

It should be equally clear that Jesus' prayer life cannot answer all the prayer needs of our day. It would create a tragic illusion to dwell simply on how Jesus can help us in our prayer life. There are two ways in which that illusion would undo much of what this book has sought to accomplish:

1. It would abandon the open and analytical approach to human experience so evident in the disciplines of historical study. The very disciplines which brought us to the rather surprising and exciting prayer life of the historical Jesus are ones that ask us always to keep part of our consciousness analytical. As we have seen, critical consciousness does not need to be reductionist or anti-spiritual. Contrary to some popular spiritual gurus, prayer and analytical thought are not opposed to one another. They can work together. If openness and critical consciousness are a part of prayer, no one model of prayer—even Jesus'—will suffice.

2. It would miss the obvious shortcomings of Jesus' prayer life relative to many pressing needs of our time. It is impossible that first century Galilee should correspond completely in its spiritual climate to America at the threshhold of the second millennium.

Several specific arenas where Jesus' prayer life does not adequately address contemporary spiritual needs deserve attention.

Contemplative prayer

The hectic pace of life today is showing itself to impoverish the spirits of many caught up in it. Many people lose track of who they are and what is important to them because of the overwhelming pressure of their daily routine. As they become aware of the toll this busy pace is taking, many people are reclaiming ancient traditions of contemplative prayer, models and exercises which give them a perspective on their hectic lives and reorient them through meditative exercises, most often alone. Contemplative prayer is proving in our day to meet very important spiritual needs by virtue of its ability to situate one in a larger history of spiritual practice, break the cycles of busy-ness, and center one's self in lasting values.

This book's search for the historical Jesus' prayer life has not shown Jesus to be involved in contemplative prayer. On the contrary, the kind of prayer in evidence in this study has been extremely socially interactive and in the middle of busy life. It is not impossible to imagine Jesus as a contemplative, but such a portrait has little or no evidentiary support.

Rather than undermine this study's effort to be rigorously analytical or engage in speculation, it is both more honest and unpretentious to con-clude that Jesus' prayer life is of little help to people interested in con-templative prayer today. The need to develop ways of praying contem-platively today is clear. Within the Bible the Lukan gospel, even with its lack of historical reliability, provides important resources. Outside of the Bible, the mystics of the Middle Ages can show ways to contemplative prayer. And beyond Christianity, eastern disciplines of prayer have grand traditions of contemplative practice.

Prayer together

As noted earlier, the social interaction inherent in Jesus' prayer had a certain openness to prayer together inasmuch as it was regularly said in the middle of an ordinary social situation and it seemed to delight in tweaking the listeners with its clever twists.

There is, on the other hand, another kind of collective prayer helpful-ly re-appearing in our day that is as helpful as the prayers of the historical Jesus. This kind of prayer which is assisting many people in growing spir-itually almost always takes the form of group ritual expression. In a rela-tively formal manner and often in a worship setting, people pray through chanting together, having communion together, davening together, or Oming together. Many of these ancient traditions of collective prayer merge those praying into one general consciousness and voice.

These new modes of praying together are indeed positive counter-balances to the highly individualized ways Americans generally express themselves. Chanting together in one way or another or having commu-nion together breaks through the "only me" prejudices of many Americans, and helps in re-connecting persons to a more tribal and com-munal sense of being together. Especially for American Protestants this renewal of praying together corrects their bias where praying alone has been overemphasized.

Jesus' highly self-critical prayers—which always seemed to be goading someone's consciousness or pushing people to examine their own person-al actions—do not help in this particular contemporary renewal of prayer.

We have seen all the ways in which Jesus' hyper-conscious prayer helps us, but this is not one of those places. Such self-criticism only inhibits people from joining in an un-selfconsious, collective expression.

Prayer in relationship to nature

Many people today are re-discovering the spiritual power of trees, rocks, sky, stars, and sun. Prayer is often enriched simply by being outside and in contact with nature.

This renewed awareness of the way nature deepens one's spiritual awareness and practice of prayer stands in some tension to a perennial Christian devaluation of nature. A number of schools of Christian thought have associated prayer in nature with a lower form of spirituality. In contra-distinction to deep medieval traditions celebrating God in nature, these tendencies within recent Christian thought have dismissed such prayer as "animist" or "pantheist."

Similarly, the rise of technology in the western world over the past two centuries has tended to see humans as dominating and controlling nature, rather than living in spiritual partnership with it. Furthermore, the dominance of the automobile and mass communications has often taken humans away from extended exposure to nature and the spiritual benefits that contact can bring.

A sense of freedom and depth has come to those who have been able to escape the grips of such anti-nature Christian spirituality and the tyranny of technology. Often the discoveries of new science have helped people return to a sense of awe about the natural universe. This re-discovery of the spiritual import of nature is basic to much post-technological spiritual vitality.

Unfortunately the prayers of the historical Jesus which this book has identified make practically no reference to the natural world. The intense social interaction of the prayers do not even allude to the stars, the trees, or the birds. So here too the prayer life of the historical Jesus does not provide a resource for spiritual renewal. The absence of nature-related prayers makes the style of prayer discovered in the historical Jesus hauntingly similar to some Christian anti-nature rhetoric and the contemporary technological dominance.

It is true that some of the teachings of the historical Jesus powerfully invoke on "the birds of the air," "the lilies of the field," "the mustard seed," and "leaven" as images of God's basileia. But the prayers of Jesus that we have discovered make no reference to this powerful spiritual realm.

Conclusion

With some notable exceptions, Jesus' surprising style of prayer promises a great deal. Although its foreign-ness at first makes it almost inaccessible, on closer examination we have discovered a number of ways that his prayer can enrich our search for a spirituality of integrity today. Although its intensity and vibrant social character were initially overwhelming, this chapter has found a number of contact points between his rigor and today's situations.

14

The Lord's Prayer Today

It is with a certain wistfulness that I now turn to one of the most obvious questions raised by this book. It is this: Since the prayer life of the historical Jesus seems not to have included the Lord's Prayer—indeed since
his prayer seems to have been very different in style than the Lord's
Prayer—what do we do with the Lord's Prayer today? What part does the
most famous and well-known prayer of Christianity play in authentic
Christian prayer, when it has been—as it has in this book—disentangled
from the prayer life of the historical Jesus?

My wistfulness comes from simultaneous realizations that: (1) the
conclusions of this book do have disturbing implications for ordinary
Christians' understanding of the Lord's Prayer; (2) for many Christians
the idea of authentic prayer is tied closely to the saying of the Lord's
Prayer as a prayer of Jesus; and (3) the character of all meaningful prayer
itself is complex and multi-faceted. I hope that all three of these realizations can be honored at the same time. I am wistful because I realize that
the brittle character of most religious consciousness and conversation
today tends to miss such subtle simultaneities.

This obvious question: "What to do with a Lord's Prayer that is not
from the historical Jesus?" points to a larger set of questions this book raises. What do we do with the body of rote and written prayers said by
Christians in a variety of settings today, when they are so different from
the prayer life of the historical Jesus sketched in this book? What do we
do with the large body of prayer material in the churches that is in dire
need of the challenging wit of Jesus' prayers? How do we estimate the
value of prayers which, although full of meaning for Christians, are strikingly out of harmony with the prayers of Jesus?

Chapter 13 proposed a whole series of ways in which the prayer life of
the historical Jesus can refresh the spirituality of contemporary searchers.
In addition, it acknowledged that although Jesus' prayer life was freshing

and creative, it does not contain all the answers to contemporary spiritual questions. This chapter proposes to address the difficult questions about contemporary use of the Lord's Prayer and other liturgical material all the while exhibiting a full appreciation both of Jesus' bold prayer style and of the many other ways of praying.

The Problem With the Lord's Prayer

Praying "the prayer Jesus taught us" today poses the following problems:

1. Obviously not all of the Lord's Prayer is from the historical Jesus. As we saw in chapters three and four, it is a blatant fiction that Jesus prayed the prayer that Christians around the world pray as his. Even if one does not immediately accept this book's thesis that the prayer is made up of a combination of prayer fragments from the historical Jesus and later additions, the fact that the prayer said in churches today is found nowhere in the gospels makes its fictional character obvious.

Clearly the gospel versions have been augmented. The traditional section "For thine is the kingdom and power and glory forever"—although one of the most beautiful parts of the prayer—is found in neither Matthew or Luke, and is clearly a later liturgical addition.

There are also important differences between the versions given by Matthew and Luke. The obvious contrast between asking forgiveness of real debts (Matthew) and sins (Luke) illustrates that the content of the Lord's Prayer said today is highly problematic. This difficulty is even more unsettling in light of the probable closeness of Matthew's "forgive us our debts" to Jesus and the preference of most churches for the Lukan "forgive us our sins/trespasses."

So the content of today's Lord's Prayer clearly does not come completely from Jesus. To pray it as "the prayer Jesus taught us" participates on some level in a jarring fiction.

2. Not only is the content contrived, the style of the Lord's Prayer differs greatly from the prayer style of the historical Jesus. Not only is the content far from assured as being from Jesus. The way Christians pray the Lord's Prayer today has little resemblance to the highly socially interactive, self-critical, and humorous prayer of Jesus himself.

The style of the Lord's Prayer is that of a collection of petitions to God, introduced by a sentence of praise. Many theologians have quite correctly noted that the Lord's Prayer could be seen as a summary of the main ideas of Jesus' teachings. But to pray a summary of Jesus' main ideas is far from the pithy and provocative prayer sentences we have discovered at the heart of Jesus' ministry. The style of the Lord's Prayer is that of a summary or collection. Jesus prayers did not summarize. They jolted, tweaked, and surprised.

3. As a memorized prayer, the Lord's Prayer obscures the socially interactive character of Jesus' own prayer. Today's Lord's Prayer is a rote recital. Jesus, on the other hand, prayed in order to interrupt routine, not to establish it. The aphoristic prayers of Jesus this book has discovered have almost nothing in common with a memorized prayer.

I do not mean to deprecate memorized prayers. They have enormous value to many people. They often create a different level of consciousness, which enables trance and other valuable states of altered consciousness. The problem here is not that memorized prayers are inferior, but rather that Jesus' prayer life thrived on surprising tweaks, not trance-like rhythms.

4. The Lord's Prayer's focus on God as Father undercuts contemporary needs for inclusive language in prayer. That the most repeated prayer in Christianity calls on God as Father, while much of Christianity is struggling to include women and women's perspectives, can be counter-productive.

Moreover, the current defense of the use of male God language in prayer misses the main intentions of Jesus praying "Abba" or "Father." As was noted in chapter five, Jesus' use of "Abba/Father" was not said in order to reinforce patriarchal authority or the male character of God. Rather, it was most likely intended to be an innovative aberration, which challenged the standard ways of thinking about God. Ironically, calling God "Mother" today may do more justice to the reforming intention of Jesus, when he prayed "Abba/Father."

5. The Lord's Prayer is almost completely devoid of concern for others. What Christians call "intercessory" prayer is not a part of the Lord's Prayer. The petitions in the Lord's Prayer are made more or less completely on behalf of those praying.

In terms of the importance of caring and praying for others—especially those in need—valued by all segments of Christianity, the Lord's Prayer is woefully lacking as a keynote of Christian prayer. Although our examination of its origin in the Q community can explain and honor why the prayer that eventually became the expanded Lord's Prayer did not contain intercessions for others, the lack of concern for others makes it less than ideal.

These five major problems with praying the Lord's Prayer as "the prayer Jesus taught us" cannot be either avoided or understated. Although some of these problems with the contemporary usefulness of the Lord's Prayer come into sharper focus through this book's proposals, they all present real challenges to contemporary Christians even without the conclusions in this book.

What Can Be Done?

What then can be done about the Lord's Prayer today?

I suggest that not just the Lord's Prayer, but Christian prayer in general today, needs to observe two principles simultaneously in order to renew contemporary spirituality:

1. New kinds of praying need to challenge traditional ways of praying both inside and outside the churches. As outlined in chapter 13, the prayer life of the historical Jesus can insure bold "new" kinds of prayer for Christians today. It can act as a challenge to conventional prayer and spiritual business as usual. It cannot carry the whole burden of renewing Christian prayer. Many other impulses from outside Christianity and from lost traditions of earlier Christianity need to help Christians re-imagine the ways they can pray.

2. Current prayer traditions which are meaningful need to be affirmed, but without them becoming the only ways of praying. The Lord's Prayer, as one such tradition, needs to be continued as one way of praying. Re-inventing prayer completely is not necessary. A number of vital traditions of prayer still exist within contemporary Christianity.

This two-edged solution needs, however, to be refined in terms of the Lord's Prayer. Since this book underscores the problems with the Lord's Prayer in the contemporary context, the way this two-edged solution applies to the Lord's Prayer needs to be carefully outlined. The first edge of the solution—the introduction of Jesus' aphoristic prayers as challenging innovations for today—has already been charted in chapter 13. How then can the Lord's Prayer as tradition be understood and valued today?

In Worship

The Lord's Prayer functions in a dramatic and meaningful way in contemporary global Christianity just because it is the only prayer that all Christians say. As such the value of the Lord's Prayer is in its unifying effect. That Christians in Borneo, Austria, Zimbabwe, Arizona, Hong Kong, and Peru all say the same prayer makes it important as a symbol of the common bonds all these Christians have.

Especially in view of the many divisive tendencies within Christianity, the fact that everyone prays the same "Lord's Prayer" is an important sign of solidarity among all Christians. Only the eucharist or communion and baptism are celebrated as unifying acts with the frequency and globality of the Lord's Prayer. Even communion and baptism have a far wider diversity of practice than does the praying of the Lord's Prayer. From this perspective, the Lord's Prayer is thus the most unifying gesture of global Christianity. It serves as a connection among many divergent groups, a source of mutual respect, and an opportunity to remain in dialogue.

In addition to the unifying character of the Lord's Prayer, it also functions, as noted above, as a relatively accurate summary of the basics of Jesus' teachings. The emphasis on the "domain" (or kingdom) of God, forgiveness, and shared bread calls Christians to attention on basic elements of the message of Jesus. Even though the prayer does not show the clear connections among these basic teachings nor does it present them in a particularly gripping manner, it does serve as a relatively adequate reminder of what Jesus stood for.

Even though the tradition of the Lord's Prayer can be affirmed as a unifier of Christians and a summary of what Jesus stands for, one major problem still remains. How can Christians pray it as "the prayer Jesus taught us" in good conscience, since it has become obvious he neither prayed nor taught it?

My suggestion is to drop the traditional introduction of the prayer as "the prayer Jesus taught us." Simply inviting people to pray the "Lord's Prayer" or the "Our Father" can suffice. These two traditionally Protestant and Roman Catholic labels for the prayer have their own integrity. The "Lord's Prayer" is an accurate description of prayer. The historical Jesus never used the title "Lord" about himself. Historians and theologians generally agree that the title "Lord" was applied to Jesus first after his death by followers who were seeking terms to do justice to the importance Jesus had for them. It was, of course, just such a group of Jesus' followers that created the Lord's Prayer after his death. Similarly the Roman Catholic designation of the prayer as the "Our Father" is wonderfully value neutral in terms of the historical Jesus. "Our Father" simply designates part of the prayer's content, not who prayed it.

Worshipful introductions to the Lord's Prayer would then go something like "And now let us pray together the 'Lord's Prayer,'" or "Let us pray together the 'Our Father.'" This sort of introduction avoids the inaccuracy or hypocrisy of the introductions which allude to the "prayer Jesus taught us."

In Private Devotion

The humor-filled, jolting prayer style of Jesus could do much to invigorate contemporary private, devotional prayer. As outlined in chapter 13, Jesus' kind of praying has enormous promise for private prayer today. But what of the Lord's Prayer today as a private devotional prayer? Given the findings of this book, how can people pray the Lord's Prayer privately?

Here again the main adjustment to be made is simply to remove the claim that the historical Jesus prayed the Lord's Prayer. In today's contexts of private prayer he Lord's Prayer has similar intrinsic values as in group worship. Praying it privately connects the person praying to all Christians around the world, since it is prayed by nearly all Christians. Praying the Lord's Prayer privately also connects the person praying to her/his particular community of prayer. And, praying the Lord's Prayer privately can be especially evocative of contemplative and altered consciousness prayer, simply by virtue of its easy repetition. Removing the claim that the Lord's Prayer comes from the historical Jesus can free it to be a valuable part of Christian tradition in its own right.

The Historical Jesus' Prayer versus Worship Today

Christian prayer in worship today is dominated by three types: written prayers, memorized prayers, and pastoral prayers. In many ways, the dominance of these prayer styles makes much Christian prayer narrow and unimaginative. So many Christian worship services oscillate lifelessly in this narrow range of expression. Most striking is that none of these three styles allows enthusiasm on the part of the worshipping community. Written prayers are simply read. Memorized prayers are recited by rote.

Pastoral prayers—although often more lively—take the expressive possibility away from the community and give it to the pastor.

This is not to suggest that all written, memorized, and pastoral prayers are unhelpful spiritually. At least one of the reasons these styles persist is that they continue to nurture some people in worship. Still the contrast between these dominant styles of community prayer and the prayer life of the historical Jesus is stark. Jesus would have never written down a prayer. He would have resisted a memorized institutionalization of words. It is almost impossible to imagine him pronouncing a long speech, much less a long prayer.

Jesus' prayer provoked responses from those listening in and those praying with him. Sometimes these responses to Jesus' short prayer jabs must have been angry, puzzled, or full of laughter. How different from people's response to written, memorized, and pastoral prayers! So Jesus' prayer stands today as a challenge to the dominant ways of praying. As noted in chapter 13, Jesus' way of praying promises to make prayer today more socially interactive, more self-critical, funnier, and more down to earth.

Again, however, the renewal of spirituality today cannot depend solely on the historical Jesus. Although his prayer does offer refreshing new departures, the dominant styles of contemporary prayer must also be challenged and enhanced by other prayer traditions. For instance, the ecstacy of sufi dancing, the expressiveness of charismatic tongues, the rigor of monastic disciplines of chant and interiority are all showing signs of breaking Christians free from the narrow dominance of written, memorized, and pastoral prayer. The prayer of the historical Jesus is only one of many different styles of prayer needed for spiritual renewal today.

15

A New Theology
of Prayer

As far as we can tell, the historical Jesus did not have a theology of prayer. There is nothing in any texts which shows Jesus reflecting on how to talk about prayer in God terms.

But the startlingly different practice of prayer by the historical Jesus does open up some new possibilities for us to think about prayer and its relationship to God. One of the main results of our encounter with Jesus' intensely socially interactive prayer is a strong awareness of how western dualism has harmed both the way we pray and the way we think about God.

There are so many ways western dualism has fragmented us and obscured our understandings. Even a cursory review of this book, however, makes the damage painfully clear. Two dualisms have been at work in us to undercut both our experience of prayer and our understanding of God. These are conceptualities which the prayer practice of the historical Jesus seems to have avoided altogether.

The two dualisms which control most Christian thinking about prayer are the body-soul split and the earth-heaven dichotomy. Since almost all of our western imagination has encouraged us to see ourselves as involved in these two dualisms, we have imagined the dynamic of prayer in one or both of the following ways:

Prayer is the means to go from the body to the soul.

Prayer is the means to go from earth to heaven.

These two ways of thinking about prayer can be visualized as in Diagram 1 (p. 129).

Within this model our experience of prayer then situates God in another obvious dualism, illustrated in Diagram 2 (p. 129).

So the universe in which we situate prayer is filled with dualisms which look something like Diagram 3 (p. 129).

In the model illustrated by Diagram 3, prayer connects us to God by taking us out of our bodies and away from the earth. If one can locate us close to God in this common way of picturing prayer, it is only our souls that are near God. We have to leave our bodied reality and earth's contingencies in order to be close to God. Prayer then becomes an experience of escaping. This, of course, happens at great cost to human wholeness. It makes prayer in part an alienating experience, in which we have to reject much of what we know, love, and are, in order to be in contact with God. In this distorted picture, God is understood as fundamentally belonging to another realm than the one we know about, struggle in, and love.

This has meant that when we pray we find ourselves making tremendous efforts to remove ourselves and escape into some other realms. The two realms into which we try to escape are the realm of the soul and the heavenly realm. If our prayer modes lend themselves to body-soul split, we try to remove ourselves from our body through a strange kind of interiorizing effort, in which we escape into a soul space so deeply interior that the body—both physical and social—becomes negligible. Or, if the way we pray is mediated by the earth-heaven split, we try to reach God by imagining we can project our voice and thoughts up to God in heaven. Through some kind of cosmic shouting or a long telephone line, we reach heaven in prayer.

Both the soulful interiorized escape and the projection of prayers into heaven take tremendous efforts of concentration and imagination. They also take an enormous toll on any unified self-understanding and the embodied self.

An Alternative Theology in the Prayer of Jesus

What is striking about the prayer we have uncovered behind and before the Lord's Prayer is how it demands engagement in the social situations of the ones (Jesus and/or his followers) who are praying. One cannot pray about forgiveness without forgiving. On an even more intensely social level, people cannot pray about forgiveness without laughing at each other's resistance to being involved in the issue at hand.

Similarly, in the style of the historical Jesus, one cannot pray about God's basileia/kingdom without mocking the claims and pretensions of Rome, and acting as if God's kingdom is already coming. One cannot pray about the holiness of God's name without challenging family idolatry. One cannot pray about one's need for bread without casting one's self on the care of others.

Diagram 1

SOUL   HEAVEN

P
R
A
Y
E
R

BODY   EARTH

Diagram 2

GOD

P
R
A
Y
E
R

WE WHO PRAY

Diagram 3

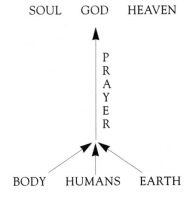

SOUL   GOD   HEAVEN

P
R
A
Y
E
R

BODY   HUMANS   EARTH

As we have seen, the prayers of the historical Jesus almost require one to pray in a group that is ready to laugh, criticize, weep, argue, and resist. It has been relatively difficult for us to feature this kind of prayer because we are so captured and alienated by the dualistic ways of western Christianity.

This kind of praying does not involve projecting one's voice to heaven. It does not require escaping into an interior realm. It meets God in the situation itself.

Just because this kind of prayer rejects the need for the heavenly or interior escape routes does not mean that it enthrones the self-contained individual by denying the importance of family, society, or the wider world. Rather this intensely social prayer thrusts one into relationship with all that surrounds the individual praying. Nor is this prayer replaceable with social interaction or group self-criticism on their own. The prayer modeled by Jesus insists on both explicit reference to God and socially interactive consciousness.

It is not enough just to pray to God, nor does it suffice to relate creatively to others. This prayer style asks that the one praying be involved in both social interaction and direct attention to God—at the same time. This is so because the character of God is discovered more thoroughly in the combination of extending one's self to others and calling on God. Giving different meaning to the notion of transcendent prayer, this style of prayer transcends the individual by requiring a relational perspective in prayer itself.

Where then is God in this kind of prayer? God is the dynamic which connects everything in this kind of prayer. Prayer becomes an experience of and with God inasmuch as one becomes connected to others through prayer. Rather than being associated with a realm so deeply interior that everything sensate disappears, or a realm so heavenly that everything earthly loses importance, God is that which connects everything on earth.

Diagram 4 illustrates this model of a prayer universe.

God is the connection between everyone. When we pray, we are participating in and recognizing the ultimacy and the intimacy of the connectedness of all that is. Prayer relates us to God by making our consciousness a part of the connectedness that is God.

This is the God we meet in the in-between. The historical Jesus seems to have prayed in a way that insisted on the reality of that which is between. His prayer did not allow him or those with him to sink into an interiority that would negate the social in-between-ness of all of life. Nor did his prayer permit the one praying to escape into heaven. The power

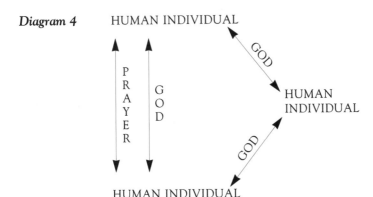

Diagram 4

of the prayer had to do with the way people reacted to one another. God came into focus in between people.

In focusing on the in-between-ness of God, one need not disown the principle that God is also in each person. There is no doubt that God lives in each person. But awareness of the in-between-ness of God helps in a provisional way to distinguish God from humans without falling into the alienation of dualism. Inasmuch as God is in between, speaking of God as "transcendent" and "other" carries meaning without breaking God's connections to humans or resorting to dualistic divisions between God and humans. In this non-dualistic, in-between vision of God, God's otherness becomes that which is between people, that which connects them. God's transcendence is that which is beyond humans inasmuch as God is between humans. God becomes the call to go beyond ourselves into the common realm connected to everyone.

From this perspective prayer is the human way of greeting and coming into relationship with the dynamic of relationality. Prayer addresses the reality of that which is not in any one person but belongs to all persons. It is like (or perhaps when one looks at recent scientific studies about the measurable effect of prayer on plants, it actually is) the electronic fields and sub-atomic connections between one supposedly discrete physical body and another.

Although there is no direct textual evidence that Jesus' prayer life extended this intense awareness of God in the in-between to non-human entities, such a logical connection does help expand understandings of both God and prayer. In other words, the in-between-ness of God can also be seen in the relationship between humans and trees and rocks as well. In this extension, God is in between people, animals, plants, water, soil, and everything that is. A partial diagram of this dynamic can be found in Diagram 5.

A picture of prayer as consciousness of the in-between-ness of God inclusive of non-human realities is illustrated in Diagram 6.

This kind of prayer would meet God not only in between people, but also in between a person and a rock. Contemplating a rock and experiencing one's connection to it would be an experience of prayer. Prayer would be the process of coming to recognize God as the connection between the one praying and the rock. Such a theology and practice of prayer not only avoids dualism, but also one of the other classic Christian errors, anthropocentrism—making everything, including God, look like and centered around humans. In contrast to anthropocentrism, such a non-human centered understanding of the universe allows the inherent value of the earth, the stars, and the animals to be affirmed.

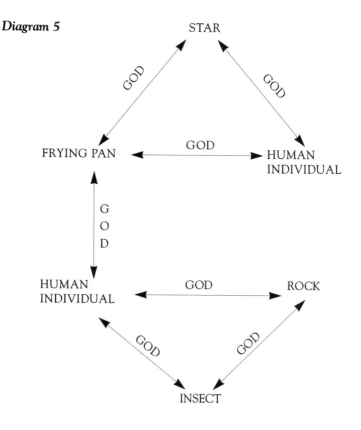

Diagram 5

As noted earlier, there is no historically reliable textual evidence that Jesus thought about or prayed in terms of God in between humans and rocks and stars. But there is at least one early Christian text which connects Jesus to this kind of view. Coming from the more legendary portions of the Gospel of Thomas, saying 77:2,3 reads: "Jesus said: Split a piece of wood, I am there. Lift up a stone, and you will find me there."

Although not from Jesus himself, this is a part of the larger near eastern wisdom tradition, which experienced God as the wisdom in all things. As the Wisdom of Solomon, also from first-century Judaism, writes: "Wisdom pervades and permeates all things" (7:16).

The saying attributed to Jesus and the perspective of the Wisdom of Solomon show that the wisdom tradition to which Jesus belonged did have a thorough-going awareness of God's in-between-ness in the non-human realm as well. It was probably as a part of the non-dualistic

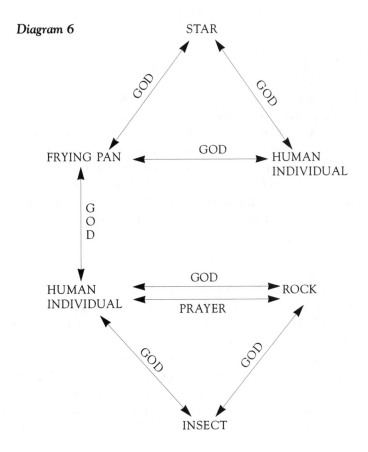

Diagram 6

character of near eastern wisdom that Jesus' prayer met God in the in-between.

Theological Traditions

There are several traditional ways of thinking about God which to some extent express the in-between-ness of God.

God as love

The author of the first epistle of John wrote that "the one who does not know love does not know God; for God is love" (4:8). In his famous work *Agape and Eros* on Christian understanding of *agape*, the primary New Testament word for love, Anders Nygren asserts that this vision of God as love was not simply a passing thought by an early Christian writer, but a fundamental dimension of the Christians vision of God.

God as love is another way of talking about the in-between-ness of God. Love can be described as the dynamic of care and affection, the most profound connection between people. To describe God as love connotes God as the loving connection between two people. In this sense, insofar as people love their "brother or sister" (1 John 3:12–16) they belong to and know God, and God is the connection between them.

In some sense this sense of God as love may not be quite as comprehensive a picture of God's in-between-ness as Jesus' aphoristic prayers. Jesus' prayers saw people connected not only in love, but also in important social systems like indebtedness and in common consciousness; while the notion of God as love seems to focus on God as the caring that connects people. In any case, the long history of God as love is another way of elucidating God's in-between-ness and placing Jesus' socially interactive prayers in a larger theological perspective.

God as Holy Spirit

The Nicene Creed confesses that the Holy Spirit "proceeds from the Father and the Son." Several medieval theologians understood this to mean that the Holy Spirit was the relationship between the first and second persons of the Christian trinity. So the Holy Spirit was seen as that of God which connected these two "persons" of the trinity.

Similarly, the notion of God's presence has been most traditionally associated with the Holy Spirit. In this way Christians have understood that when they speak of God's presence in their lives, they are referring to the Holy Spirit. In her systematic theology, *She Who Is*, Elizabeth Johnson has mapped out very thoroughly how this presence of the Holy Spirit is very much like the presence of the biblical personage of Sophia, or holy "Wisdom" who as we noted above "pervades and permeates all things."

This Holy Spirit presence both between the first two persons of the trinity and among humans is very close to the in-between-ness of God evident in the prayer life of the historical Jesus. Although the doctrine of the Holy Spirit was developed several centuries after the historical Jesus, one can understand his evocation of a divine presence between people as the presence of what came later to be called the Holy Spirit.

God as incarnate

Orthodox Christian theology has affirmed that God was "incarnate" in Jesus Christ. In Latin the word "incarnate" means literally "enfleshed." The notion of God's incarnation in Jesus was that God became enfleshed in Jesus Christ. That is, Jesus Christ was the presence of God in the flesh. Among many others, theologians Hans Kung and Jurgen Moltmann have emphasized that this classic Christian doctrine of the incarnation does not refer only to God being enfleshed and present in one individual. Rather the incarnation of God in Jesus Christ becomes for Christians an affirmation that God is always present in human history. Jewish theologian Jacob Neusner is correct in pointing out that the Jewish faith shares this understanding of the incarnation of God in its affirmation of God's activity in human history.

The incarnation of God, then, is another way of talking about meeting God in the in-between in a non-dualistic way. An incarnate God is one who is present in the interactions of human history. As incarnate, God is in the midst of people. It is true that the expression "the enfleshment of God" to a certain extent pre-supposes that God is not flesh, but some kind of soul or heavenly presence, and hence the phrase has some dualistic overtones. But the way this tradition of theological interpretation has developed in the works of Kung, Neusner, and Moltmann comes very close to the way Jesus' prayer life evoked a divine presence in the midst of human critique, humor, challenge, and care.

Conclusion

Jesus' prayer life, as uncovered in the complex search undertaken in this book, thrusts the possibility of prayer into the hot mix of personal give and take. The way he made himself open and vulnerable to others, the way he challenged everyone from Roman authorities to family members to re-orient themselves then and there to what he had said in prayer, the way he pushed himself and others to bring themselves into the immediacy of God's domain—all these envisioned and depended on a God who was present in between people.

His practice of prayer then radically derailed the alienating splits of body-mind, earth-heaven, and God-human. Prayer tuned into a completely non-dualized divine presence for him. It awaited divine power as humans laughed with one another, criticized one another, and pushed one another forward. This prayer of the historical Jesus, then, not only offers the range of enrichments to prayer discussed in chapter 13, it also breaks through toward a kind of praying that holds mind and body, earth and heaven, God and humans together.

16
Postmodern Postscript

There is no absolute rationale. All of what anyone thinks is contingent. Such basic self-consciousness applies both to this book itself and to the historical Jesus. Neither is the absolute answer.

Although the self-discipline of this study is obvious from its unpretentious results and from its complex methods in getting at what many people would consider the obvious, it is important to further qualify the results.

In keeping with the disciplines associated with analytical biblical studies in our day, this book has meant to be ruthlessly devoted to an unsentimental and vigorous search for the historical Jesus' own prayer life. But it must be acknowledged that the field of contemporary biblical studies is also a product of culturally relative disciplines.

So although the rigor of contemporary biblical studies has been honestly applied in the service of a persistent logic in this study, I am aware that there are other logics, whose rigor is strong and whose conclusions about this subject matter are different. For instance, to my more orthodox friends and readers whose logic has the discipline of working within a set of doctrinal standards I need to state my appreciation for the way they also work in a disciplined manner. Similarly, to my more eclectic friends and readers, I also grant that what often seems to me an arbitrary way of relating to biblical texts usually does have its own logic within their life.

Those of us who have devoted much of the last two decades of our scholarship to historical Jesus studies are acutely aware of our own relativity. For instance, although the public at large probably does not know this, we scholars are keenly aware that the most well-known historical Jesus scholar of the modern era, Albert Schweitzer, disagreed at the beginning of the twentieth century almost entirely with what I have called the late twentieth-century consensus about Jesus as a sage. That Schweitzer's primary data were almost exclusively material that we now exclude from the core of Jesus' teachings is at least ironic. It is true that some of us think that if Schweitzer had lived to study the material from the Gospel of Thomas and Q that we now have, he might have come to other conclusions. But the primary point remains that even the disciplined logic and methods of this book in the hands of a much greater scholar and human being, Albert Schweitzer, resulted in strikingly different conclusions.

In a final relativizing acknowledgement, it is important to know that I as author am not just a biblical scholar. I am also an intensely devoted ultra-liberal Christian. As both a teacher in higher education and a United Methodist pastor, I have invested myself in both the institutions and renewal of Christianity. Although I have worked hard at applying the methods of critical biblical studies to the material in this book, my liberal Christian commitment must have colored my interpretations in some ways.

Having conceded all of this in a thoroughly post-modern perspective, I nonetheless make one final plea for considering this book's proposals seriously. Even without adopting all of its assumptions, the reader can see how this book has followed a disciplined logic to surprising conclusions. The prayer life of the historical Jesus which has emerged is not even close to what I had hoped it would be when this study began some fifteen years ago. Nor do I particularly recommend this prayer life of Jesus as the solution to everyone's difficulties in praying today. Even as I acknowledge the relativity of my perspective and the inevitability of my biases, I ask that the reader recognize that the results I have come to are neither totally comfortable nor quite as expected for me.

May the reader beware then both of this book's implicit biases and of its surprising results. My hope is that the awareness they generate will deepen the reader's own understanding and the reader's own prayer.

RECOMMENDED READING

Ancient Sources

These two books are excellent collections of the actual documents of early Christianity with brief introductions. *The Complete Gospels* volume is a stunning collection of twenty-two different early Christian gospels within and outside the Christian Bible. The Robinson volume contains all of the documents discovered at Nag Hammadi.

Miller, Robert J., ed. *The Complete Gospels: Annotated Scholars Version*. Rev. and exp. ed. Sonoma, CA: Polebridge Press, 1994.

Robinson, James M., ed. *The Nag Hammadi Library*. 3rd rev. ed. San Francisco: Harper and Row, 1988.

The New Testament

The following books all directly relate to particular topics within the New Testament discussed in this book. The clearest and broadest introductions to the critical study of the New Testament are Stevan Davies' book and Burton Mack's work on *Who Wrote the New Testament*.

Corley, Kathleen. *Private Women, Public Meals: Social Conflict in the Synoptic Tradition*. Peabody, MA: Hendrickson, 1993.

Davies, Stevan L. *New Testament Fundamentals*. Santa Rosa, CA: Polebridge Press, 1994.

Mack, Burton L. *Who Wrote the New Testament? The Making of the Christian Myth*. San Francisco: HarperSanFrancisco, 1995.

Mack, Burton L. *A Myth of Innocence: The Gospel of Mark and Christian Origins*. Philadelphia: Fortress Press, 1988.

Riley, Gregory J. *Resurrection Reconsidered: Thomas and John in Controversy*. Minneapolis: Fortress Press, 1995.

Schussler Fiorenza, Elisabeth, ed., *Searching the Scriptures: A Feminist Introduction*. New York: Crossroad, 1993.

Schussler Fiorenza, Elisabeth, ed., *Searching the Scriptures: A Feminist Commentary*. New York: Crossroad, 1994.

Smith, Dennis and Hal Taussig, *Many Tables: The Eucharist in the New Testament and Worship Today*. Philadelphia: Trinity Press International, 1990.

The Historical Jesus

Of the works listed below, *The Five Gospels* and *The Acts of Jesus* volumes provide a comprehensive review of the work of the Jesus Seminar on the historical reliability of early Christian literature about Jesus. Crossan's book on *The Historical Jesus* is the most comprehensive and scholarly. Borg's *Meeting Jesus Again* ... is an exceptionally well-written introduction to the subject for lay people.

Borg, Marcus J. *Jesus: A New Vision*. San Francisco: Harper and Row, 1987.

Borg, Marcus J. *Meeting Jesus Again for the First Time*. San Francisco: HarperSan Francisco, 1994.

Bornkamm, Gunther. *Jesus of Nazareth*. San Francisco: Harper and Row, 1960

Crossan, John Dominic. *The Historical Jesus: The Life of a Mediterranean Jewish Peasant*. San Francisco: HarperCollins, 1991.

Crossan, John Dominic. *Jesus: A Revolutionary Biography*. San Francisco: HarperSanFrancisco, 1994.

Crossan, John Dominic. *The Cross That Spoke: The Origins of the Passion Narrative*. San Francisco: Harper and Row, 1988.

Crossan, John Dominic. *Who Killed Jesus*. San Francisco: HarperSanFrancisco, 1995.

Funk, Robert W., Roy W. Hoover and the Jesus Seminar. *The Five Gospels: The Search for the Authentic Words of Jesus*. San Francisco: HarperSanFrancisco, 1997.

Funk, Robert W. and the Jesus Seminar, *The Acts of Jesus*. San Francisco: HarperSanFrancisco, 1998.

Funk, Robert W. *Honest to Jesus: Jesus for a New Millenium*. San Francisco: HarperCollins, 1996.

The Jesus Movements

Except for Mack's very readable *The Lost Gospel*, the books in this category tend to be relatively scholarly in tone.

Downing, F. Gerald, *Cynics and Christian Origins*. Edinburgh: T & T Clark, 1992.

Kloppenborg, John S. *The Formation of Q: Trajectories in Ancient Wisdom Collections*. Philadelphia: Fortress Press, 1987.

Kloppenborg, John S., Marvin W. Meyer, Stephen J. Patterson, Michael G. Steinhauser, *Q Thomas Reader*. Sonoma, CA: Polebridge Press, 1990.

Mack, Burton L. *The Lost Gospel: The Book of Q and Christian Origins*. San Francisco: HarperSanFrancisco, 1993.

Fictional Gospels about the Historical Jesus

Carse's 'gospel' is an creative and original portrait of Jesus in the ancient gospel form, but all the material is from Carse. *The Gospel of Jesus* is a compilation of different materials from various early Christian gospels which forms a portrait of the historical Jesus.

Carse, James P., *The Gospel of the Beloved Disciple*. San Francisco: Harper SanFrancisco, 1997.

Funk, Robert W. and the Jesus Seminar, *The Gospel of Jesus According to the Jesus Seminar*. Santa Rosa: Polebridge Press, 1999.

Other Works Relevant or Cited

Charlesworth, James H. with Mark Harding and Mark Kiley. *The Lord's Prayer and Other Prayer Texts from the Greco-Roman Era*. Valley Forge, PA: Trinity Press International, 1994.

Johnson, Elizabeth, *She Who Is: The Mystery of God in Feminist Theological Discourse*. New York: Crossroad, 1993.

Nygren, Anders: *Eros and Agape*, London: 1960.

Schaberg, Jane. *The Illegitimacy of Jesus: A Feminist Theological Interpretation of the Birth Narratives*. New York: Crossroad, 1990.

SUBJECT AND AUTHOR INDEX

SCRIPTURE INDEX

Hebrew Scriptures

Early Christian Literature